CW00506181

A General Theory of Magic

A General Theory
of Magic

by

MARCEL MAUSS

translated from the French by
Robert Brain

Routledge & Kegan Paul
London and Boston

First published in Sociologie et Anthropologie
© *Presses Universitaires de France 1950*
This translation
first published 1972
by Routledge & Kegan Paul Ltd
Broadway House, 68–74 Carter Lane,
London EC4V 5EL and
9 Park Street,
Boston, Mass. 02108, U.S.A.
Printed in Great Britain by
C. Tinling & Co. Ltd, London and Prescot
© *Robert Brain 1972*

ISBN 0 7100 7338 0

Contents

Foreword

by David Pocock
School of African and Asian Studies
University of Sussex

In introducing Dr Brain's excellent translation I am acutely conscious that Professor Lévi-Strauss has not only written about *Théorie de la magie* at some length but also made it the occasion for a major, if early, statement of position.[1] Because this important document has not yet been translated I believe that I shall do the reader of the present work more service by drawing his attention to it rather than attempting something in the nature of an original essay. I shall write of Mauss's *Theory of Magic* in the perspective of Lévi-Strauss's own achievement which, in my opinion, gives it retrospectively its significance for the modern reader.

It may seem paradoxical to say that the importance of the present work is that it contributes to the dissolution of 'magic' as a category, nevertheless this is the claim made for it. The need for such an act of dissolution is to be found in the earlier history of ethnology.

Criticisms of social Darwinism in the nineteenth century are easily made and, in the process, many of the still relevant achievements of the period are neglected. One of the most important of these, at a time when notions of 'enlightenment' and 'progress' threatened to divide humanity along what today we would call 'racialist' lines according to innate capacity, was that the application to primitive societies of the theory of evolution re-established the fundamental human unity. If it now seems to us absurd that certain societies should have been thought of as representing stages in the evolution of the human species, we should remember that this was the price paid for the renewed belief in the unity of that species and the potential for change in the societies concerned.

Few theories are pure in their application and it should not surprise us if writers of that time occasionally sinned against the conception of unity by imputing, particularly in the area which they thought of as the supernatural, modes of thought which, if true, would as effectively have cut the primitive off from communication with the modern as a genetic difference would preclude inter-breeding.

The vice is not dead: some modern accounts of non-European societies, again especially in the area of 'religion', 'magic' and the like, seem to rest on assumptions about human nature which would not stand the test of application to ourselves. Indeed sometimes it seems that the primitive is to be defined as that about which any nonsense can be believed. Modern writers have less excuse than their forebears: they, for the most part, shared beliefs in, or derived from, a revealed religion which, but for the labours of their missionary brethren, was indeed closed to the majority of mankind.

'Magic' was perhaps even more prone to this treatment than 'religion'. The ethnologists of the nineteenth century knew what they, at least, meant by the latter; magic on the other hand was a peculiar and alien phenomenon and its persistence in sections of European society only heightened the scholar's sense of estrange-ment. Much of the theoretical discussion which preceded Mauss's work had for its effect not so much that of overcoming the apparent division between those who believed and those who did not (i.e. the ethnologists themselves) as of reinforcing it. Thus it comes about, for example, that we learn more about Sir James Frazer's beliefs about 'magic' than we understand about the examples which he cites.

This intrusion of the subjective is not bad in that it is inevitable; it is common to all the social sciences. However, consciousness of it imposes upon them all the perpetual task of re-examining in relation to the facts the most tried and accepted categories of their apparatus. If categorical distinctions of the Western mind are found upon examination to impose distinctions upon (and so falsify) the in-tellectual universes of other cultures then they must be discarded, or, as I have put it, dissolved. I believe 'magic' to be one such category and need only cite here by way of evidence the fact that it is perpetually opposed to 'religion' and 'science' in our literature.

Marcel Mauss certainly had no such work of demolition in mind, although I seem to see in his two concluding paragraphs some hint of an awareness that his researches had led him further than his original intent. Certainly the modern reader can derive from Mauss's wide-ranging survey of the facts and his many profound insights the materials for a further advance.

In his *Introduction* Professor Lévi-Strauss reminds us that if we are to do justice to Mauss we must remember the date at which the *Theory of Magic* was published.[2]

> It was at a time when comparative ethnology had not yet been abandoned, largely at the instigation of Mauss himself, and as he was to write in the *Essay on the Gift*: 'That constant comparison in which everything is mixed and where institutions lose all local colour and documents their savour.' Only later did he devote himself to drawing attention to societies 'which truly represent the *maxima*, the excesses, which better allow the facts to be seen than those in which, although no less essential, they remain small and undeveloped.'

This is to compare Mauss with himself and certainly no one would seek to displace the *Essay on the Gift* as his masterpiece. Nevertheless I, having given the *Theory of Magic* a role in retrospect, wonder whether its contribution to the work of dissolution does not lie in the fact that it does cover so wide a range of material. Professor Lévi-Strauss himself appears to be partly of this mind when he defends Mauss, and Durkheim also, from the common criticism alleging that they 'were wrong ... to bring together notions borrowed from widely separated regions of the world and to constitute them as a category.' The same author continues: 'Despite all the local differences it seems certain that *mana, wakan, orenda* represent explanations of the same type; it is therefore legitimate to constitute the type, to attempt to classify and to analyse it.'

It is upon this assimilation of geographically distinct notions that Professor Lévi-Strauss is able to advance the proposition:[3]

> conceptions of the *mana* type are so frequent and so widespread that we should ask ourselves if we are not confronted with a permanent and universal form of thought which . . . being a function of a certain situation of the mind in the face of things, must appear each time that this situation is given.

Lévi-Strauss then cites both the example of the Nambikwara who, on being introduced to cattle, designated them by a term very close in its connotation to *manitou* and the example of French words used for essentially mysterious objects. From these he passes to the observation that in our own society such terms are fluid and spontaneous whereas elsewhere they constitute the base for considered and official systems of explanation, a role which we reserve for science.[4]

Lévi-Strauss's argument leads him finally to see the *mana* type notion as pure symbol or as having *zero symbolic value*: a formulation analogous to the linguistic zero phoneme. This analysis, which carries us beyond the category 'magic', is explicitly related to the contribution of Mauss who 'was one of the very first to denounce the insufficiency of psychology and traditional logic and to disrupt their rigid frames by revealing other forms of thought, apparently "alien to our adult European understanding." '[5] Lévi-Strauss's first and simplest formulation runs as follows:[6]

> Always and everywhere notions of this (*mana*) type intervene, somewhat as algebraic symbols, to represent a value of indeterminate meaning (*signification*), which being itself empty of meaning (*sens*) is therefore susceptible to the reception of any meaning (*sens*) whatsoever. Its unique function is to make good a discrepancy between signifier and signified, or, more exactly, to draw attention to the fact that in certain circumstances, on a certain occasion or in certain of their manifestations, a relation of inadequacy exists between signified and signifier to the detriment of the anterior relation of complementarity.

This is an important step: it does not dissolve the concept 'magic' so much as, so to speak, cut the ground from beneath it. A field of explanation is opened in which what we call 'magic'—pre-eminently an activity—is only one of, and of the same order as, many symbolic actions which overcome the discrepancies of thought. Rituals *do* what words cannot *say*: in *act* black and white can be mixed; the young man is made an adult; spirit and man can be combined or separated at will. Indeed actions speak louder than words.

Let me give an example of a very simple magical act which I have observed in Gujarat, in western India. A Hindu by accident brushes against, touches an Untouchable. To free himself from the consequent pollution he then touches a Muslim. The structure of the situation is as follows. The Muslim is not a Hindu, he is outside the caste system and the world of purity and impurity as are all non-Hindus. Nevertheless, he is given a place in the Hindu caste hierarchy in the village. The Untouchable, on the other hand, is of his nature an essential element in the system; he personifies the negative pole of impurity, an impurity, let us note, which at the level of thought, embraces Muslims, Christians, etc. The Untouchable's function in the system is to be excluded from its activities; to be treated as an outsider. There is then, so to speak, an absurdity in the system: the outsider is thought of as an insider, and the insider is treated as an outsider.

It is against this absurdity that we now observe the Hindu who has by accident touched the Untouchable. It is like a game of tag—he has equated himself with the Untouchable. He frees himself from this association by deliberately touching the Muslim whose contradictory nature—insider/outsider, pure/impure—provides the conduit for a restoration of normality: the Hindu and Untouchable are again separate. It is important that I stress that it is only on this occasion and for this purpose that the contradiction of the Muslim's position is used. In certain circumstances he may be recognized as a Muslim, in the majority of circumstances he is assimilated in the Hindu caste system, one or the other. Only in the circumstances that I have described is his double and contradictory value recognized.

One major criticism of Mauss's work is to be found in Lévi-Strauss's discussion. It is worth reporting at length not only because of its relevance to the present text, but also because it touches upon a continuing tendency in modern anthropology.

The anthropologist inevitably works with the categories of his own culture and consciously refines them through the experience of others. He may, and sometimes does, imagine that his categories are perfectly matched in the cultures which he observes; thus *they* are believed to practise 'magic' as he supposes it to be. From this it is an easy and dangerous step to imagine that the entire phenomenon is now accessible to his empathic understanding. Ironically an unreflective empiricism is thus transformed into simple-minded subjectivism. Because of this tendency I take the opportunity of translating Lévi-Strauss's critique at length.[7]

We refuse to accompany Mauss when he looks for the origin of the notion of *mana* in an order of realities other than the relations which it helps to construct: the order of sentiments, volitions and beliefs which are, from the point of view of a sociological explanation either epiphenomena or mysteries, in any case extrinsic to the field of investigation. This pursuit is, to our mind, the reason why an enquiry in itself so rich and penetrating, so full of illuminations, falls short and ends deceptively. In the final account *mana* is but 'the expression of social sentiments which have been formed, sometimes fatefully and universally, sometimes fortuitously in relation to certain things, chosen for the greater part in an arbitrary manner. . . .' But notions of sentiment, fatality, fortuity and arbitrary are not scientific notions. They do not throw light upon the phenomena which they claim to explain, they participate in them. We can see that in one case at least, the notion of *mana* does present those characteristics of mysterious power and secret force which Durkheim and Mauss attribute to it: it plays just such a role in their own system. There truly, *mana* is *mana*. At the same time one wants to know whether their theory of *mana* is anything other than an imputation to native thought of properties which were implied by the very particular role that the idea of *mana* was called upon to play in their own.

It would be peculiarly inauspicious to close on a negative note a foreword to a work of this nature. That the leading ethnologist of our time should lean with such weight upon a fifty-year-old argument is as good a testimony as one could wish to its vitality. One can on occasion become irritated with Mauss as with a contemporary and it is Lévi-Strauss himself who has insisted in the same *Introduction* upon the astonishing *modernity* of the mind of Marcel Mauss.

Notes

1 'Introduction a l'œuvre de Marcel Mauss' in Marcel Mauss, *Sociologie et anthropologie*, Presses Universitaires de France, Paris, 1950.
2 Op. cit., p. xli.
3 Op. cit., pp. xlii–xliii.
4 Op. cit., pp. xliii–xliv.
5 Op. cit., p. li.
6 Op. cit., p. xliv.
7 Op. cit., p. xlv.

Prologue

Up to now, the history of religions has consisted of a blurred bundle of ideas. We already have a wealth of authentic and instructive facts which will one day furnish a science of religions with abundant material. Unfortunately these facts are haphazardly classified, under vague headings; sometimes their presentation is spoiled by slipshod language. Words such as religion and magic, prayer and incantation, sacrifice and offering, myth and legend, god and spirit are interchanged indiscriminately. The science of religion has no scientific terminology. Nothing but gain would result from establishing one. However, our aim is not only to define words, but to set up natural classes of facts and, once we have established them, to attempt an analysis which will be as explanatory as possible. These definitions and explanations will provide us with scientific notions—that is, clear ideas about things and their inter-relation.

We have proceeded along these lines in our study of sacrifice. We chose it as a subject of study because it seemed to us to be one of the most typical of all religious actions. We decided to explain the mechanism and also the apparent multiplicity of functions which the rite had to serve, once it had been set up; in fact we tried to justify the importance of its position in the whole religious system.

The first problem led to others, including those we are dealing with now. We came to realize, during our study of sacrifice, the real nature of the rite. Its universality, its constancy, the logic of its development—all this gave it, in our eyes, a kind of inevitability, far superior to the authority of legal convention that seemed sufficient to impose observance of it. Because of this, sacrifice and, as an extension, rites in general, appeared to us deeply rooted in social life. On the other hand, we considered that the mechanism of sacrifice would not be explained except through a logical application of the idea of the sacred; we assumed this to be so and made it the starting point of our studies. We held, furthermore, in our conclusions, that sacred things, involved in sacrifice, did not constitute a system of propagated illusions, but were social, consequently real. We found, finally, that sacred things were considered to provide an inexhaustible source of power, capable of producing effects which were infinitely special and infinitely varied. In so far as we could consider sacrifice to be a rite which could be regarded as representative of all the rest, we came to the general conclusion that the basic idea of all ritual—which was to become the major theme of our enquiries—was this idea of the sacred.

However, this initial generalization was found to be wanting; we had unearthed it while studying an institution which was too special and which had not yet been stripped of its differential characteristics. We had treated it solely as a religious rite, not simply as a rite. Was our induction valid only for religious rites, on the religious quality of which it depended? Or could we extend it to all kinds of rites, whether they were religious or not? First of all we had to see if there were rites other than religious ones. This is implicitly admitted in the way people currently talk of magical rites. Magic includes, in fact, a whole group of practices which we seem to compare with those of religion. If we are to find any other rites apart from those which are nominally religious, we shall find them here.

In order to verify and broaden the conclusions of our researches, we decided to make magic the subject of a second study. If we succeed in finding ideas related to a concept of the sacred, as the basis of magic, we shall be justified in extending the conclusions which we proved to be true for sacrifice to all kinds of mystical and traditional techniques. That is because magical rites are precisely those which, at first glance, seem to be imbued with the least amount of sacred power. One can easily imagine the fascination of these studies which were to lead to a theory of ritual in general. Nevertheless our ambitions did not cease here. At the same time we were making our way towards a theory of the idea of the sacred; that was due to the fact that, while we found ideas of the same order functioning in magic, we had gained quite a different image of its meaning, its generality and also its origin.

At the same time this raised a serious difficulty and as a result we were encouraged to embark on this study. As we have said before, the idea of the sacred is a social idea, that is, it is a product of collective activities; moreover, the prohibition or prescription of certain things seemed to be in fact the result of a kind of entente. We were forced to conclude, therefore, that magical practices which derive from this idea or a similar one, are social facts in the same sense that religious rites are social facts. But this is not the normal aspect presented by magical rites. Since they are practised by individuals who are outside the social group, who act in their own interests or in the interest of other individuals, or in their name, these magical rites seem to require much more ingenuity and *savoir-faire* from their practitioners. In these circumstances, how is it that magic can derive from a collective idea such as our notion of the sacred, and exploit it? Here we are faced with a dilemma: either magic is a collective idea or the notion of the sacred is an individual one. In order to solve this problem we shall have to discover whether magical rites take place in a social milieu, because if we are able to discover in magic the presence of such a milieu, we shall be able to show then that an idea of a social nature similar to that of the sacred can function in magic; it would then only be a matter of revealing that this idea did function there.

This is the third gain we promised to make from these researches. We shall pass from observing the mechanism of the rite to the study of the milieu of these rites, since it is only in the milieu, where magical rites occur, that we can find the *raison d'être* of those practices performed by individual magicians.

We shall not, therefore, analyse a series of magical rites, but that ensemble of magic which is the immediate milieu of magical rites. An attempt at such a description may then allow us to resolve the very controversial question of the relation between magic and religion. For the moment we are not banning any consideration of this problem, but we do not wish to dwell on it, since we are anxious to attain our ends. We wish to understand magic itself, before we explain its history. We shall leave aside for the moment— keeping it for a future study—any contribution these researches could make, in the form of new facts, to religious sociology. More-over, we have been tempted to quit the limited sphere of our usual preoccupations and make a contribution to sociological studies in general, by showing how, as far as magic is concerned, isolated individuals can affect social phenomena.

The subject we have assigned ourselves demands different methods from those we used in our study of sacrifice. It is not possible here, or rather it would not be fruitful, to proceed by the analysis—even a very complete analysis—of a number—even a large number—of magical ceremonies. In fact, magic is not to be compared with sacrifice; it is one of those collective customs which cannot be named, described, analysed without the fear that one may lose the feeling that they have any reality, form or function of their own. Magic is an institution only in the most weak sense; it is a kind of totality of actions and beliefs, poorly defined, poorly organized even as far as those who practise it and believe in it are concerned. As a result we cannot know *a priori* its limits, and we are in no position to choose, with any certainty, those typical facts which could be said to represent the totality of magical facts. We must first make a kind of inventory of these facts, which will give us an opportunity of limiting—at least to some extent—the field of our researches. In other words, we ought not to try and consider independently a series of isolated rites, but consider all those things which constitute magic as a whole; we must, in sum, begin by defining and describing it. In the analysis which follows, we shall not be guided by the successive moments of a rite. The interest lies not in the plan or composition of the rite, but in the nature of magic's working methods, independently of their application: the interest lies in the beliefs involved in magic, the feelings it provokes and the agents who perform it.

chapter one

Sources and Historical Background

For a long time, magic has been a matter for speculation. However, the studies of ancient philosophers, alchemists and theologians were purely practical in nature and belong more to the history of magic itself than to the history of those scientific studies which have been devoted to the subject. The first in this list is the work of the brothers Grimm, which inaugurated a long series of studies of which our researches are a continuation.

Today we have good monographs on most of the important magical themes. Data have been collected both from a historical as well as an analytical point of view, and we can now call on a whole range of knowledge. On the other hand a certain number of theoretical ideas have become established, including the notion of 'survival' and that of 'sympathetic magic'.

Our immediate predecessors are the scholars of the anthropological school who have already produced a sufficiently coherent theory of magic. E. B. Tylor, in his *Primitive Culture*, deals with the subject twice. He first associates magical demonology with primitive animism. In his second volume he mentions—and he is one of the first to do so—'sympathetic magic'; this term covers those magical rites which follow the so-called laws of sympathy. Like produces like; contact results in contagion; the image produces the object itself; a part is seen to be the same as the whole. Tylor's main aim was to show that these rites played a role in the system of survivals. In fact, Tylor offers no other explanation of magic than the one provided by his general theory of animism. George Wilken and Sidney Hartland also studied magic: the former in connexion with animism and shamanism, the latter in relation to life tokens, equating sympathetic magic with those bonds which are said to exist between a man and the object or being with which his life is bound up.

With J. G. Frazer and W. Lehmann we finally have genuine theories of magic. Frazer's ideas, as they are set out in the second edition of *The Golden Bough*, provide, as we believe, the clearest expression of a whole tradition to which the works of Tylor, Sir Alfred Lyall, F. B. Jevons, A. Lang and H. Oldenberg all belong. Despite divergent opinions in matters of detail, all these writers agree in calling magic a kind of pre-science; and as it is the basis of Frazer's theories we shall begin by discussing this aspect. As far as Frazer is concerned, magical actions are those which are destined to produce special effects through the application of two laws of sympathetic magic—the law of similarity and the law of contiguity. He formulates these in the following way: 'Like produces like; objects which have been in contact, but since ceased to be so, continue to act on each other at a distance after the physical contact has been severed.' One might add, as a corollary: 'The part is to the whole as the image is to the represented object.' Thus the definitions of the anthropological school tend to confuse 'magic' with sympathetic magic'. Frazer's ideas are dogmatic in this regard; he expresses no doubts and offers no exceptions to his rules. Sympathy is a sufficient and inevitable feature of magic; all magical rites are sympathetic and all sympathetic ritual is magical. It is true that magicians perform ritual which is akin to religious prayers and sacrifice—and not always in parody or imitation. It is also true that priests in a number of societies have a remarkable predisposition towards magical practices. But these facts, we are told, are but the encroachments of recent times and should be excluded from our general definition, which is only concerned with pure magic.

From this first proposition it is possible to deduce others. In the first place magical rites act upon their object directly without any mediation by a spiritual agent; moreover, their effectiveness is automatic. However, as far as these two properties are concerned, the first is not universal, since it is admitted that magic—in its degenerate phase, when it became contaminated by religion—has borrowed figures of gods and demons from religion. The truth of the second proposition is not affected by this, since in the cases where we have intermediaries, the magical rite acts on them in the same way as it does on external phenomena; magic forces and constrains, while religion conciliates. This last property, which seems to distinguish magic from religion in every case where there is a temptation to confuse the two, remains—according to Frazer—the most permanent general feature of magic.

This theory involves a hypothesis of much wider import. Magic, thus defined, becomes the earliest form of human thought. It must have once existed in its pure state; mankind, originally, thought only in magical terms. The predominance of magical ritual in primitive cults and folklore provide—so it is thought—strong proof in support of this argument. Moreover, it is maintained that these magical states of mind still exist among a few central Australian tribes whose totemic rites are purely magical in character. Magic is, therefore, the foundation of the whole mystical and scientific universe of primitive man. It is the first stage in the evolution of the human mind which he determined—or even conjectured. Religion grew up out of the failures and mistakes of magic. Originally man unhesitatingly expressed his ideas and their associations in concrete form. He thought he would create those things suggested to him by his mind; he imagined he was master of the external world in the same way as he was master of his own movements. But he finally realized that the world was resisting his attempts to do so. Immediately he endowed his universe with mysterious powers, of the kind he once arrogated to himself. Once upon a time man himself was god, now he peopled the world with gods. These gods were no longer bent to his will, but he attached himself to them in worship, through sacrifice and prayer. Frazer, it is true, presents these hypotheses with many careful reservations; nevertheless, he is determined to stick to them. He rounds the theory off by explaining how the human mind, following on from religion, moved off in the direction of science. Once man became capable of noting the errors of religion he returned to a straightforward application of the principle of causality. But from this time onwards it is a matter of experimental causality and not magical causality. Later we shall return in detail to different aspects of this theory.

Lehmann's work is a study in psychology, prefaced by a short history of magic. He begins by pointing out some contemporary facts. Magic, which he defines as 'the practising of superstitions'—that is, 'beliefs which are neither religious nor scientific'—exists in our society in the observable forms of spiritualism and occultism. He attempts, therefore, to analyse the principal experiences of spirits through the processes of experimental psychology and he manages to discover in it (and also, as a corollary, in magic) illusions prejudices and errors of perception caused by these anticipatory phenomena.

All these studies betray one common feature, or error. No attempt has been made to enumerate fully the different categories of magical facts and, as a result, it is doubtful whether, at this stage, it is possible to propose a scientific scheme which could embrace the whole subject. The only attempt so far made—by Frazer and Jevons—to circumscribe magic, has been spoilt by the authors' prejudices. They used so-called 'typical data', assumed the existence of a period in the past when magic existed in its purest state, and then reduced the whole to facts of sympathetic magic. However, they failed to prove the legitimacy of their selection. They ignored a considerable body of practices which are called magical by all those who perform the rites and also those who observe them; as well as incantations and rituals involving demons, properly so called. If one ignores the old definitions and sets up in their place a class of ideas and practices which are so narrowly limited that they exclude magical phenomena which only *seem* to be magical, we must again ask how it is possible to explain those illusions which have induced so many people to accept facts as magical which, by themselves, are not. We are still waiting in vain for an explanation of this. We may also be told that the phenomena of sympathetic magic form a natural and independent class of facts which it is important to distinguish. This may be so. In this case we should need proof that they have produced expressions, images and social attitudes which are sufficiently distinct for us to be able to accept that they clearly do form a separate class from the rest of magic. We, it should be added, believe that this is not so. In any case, it would then be necessary to make it clear that we were being given only a theory of sympathetic actions, not a theory of magic in general. In fact, nobody so far has been able to produce a clear, complete and wholly satisfactory idea of magic which we could make use of. As a result we are reduced to providing one for ourselves.

In order to succeed in this aim, we determined not to restrict our studies to one or two magical systems, but to consider the largest number possible. We do not believe that an analysis of a single system, however well chosen, would be sufficient to deduce laws, applicable to all magical phenomena, since our uncertainty about the actual boundaries of magic leads us to doubt whether we could find the totality of magical phenomena in one magical system. On the other hand, we propose studying as many heterogeneous systems as possible. In doing so we may be able to establish whether magic— no matter how it varies in relation to other categories of social phenomena from culture to culture—involves, in some degree, the same basic elements and whether it is on the whole everywhere the same. Above all we must make parallel studies of magical systems of both primitive and differentiated societies. In the former we shall find the most perfect form, the basic phenomena of magic from which others derive; in the latter, with their more complex organization and more distinct institutions, we shall find data which are more intelligible to us and which will provide insights into the functioning of the primitive systems.

We have taken care to use only the most reliable material which gives a complete coverage of magic in the society concerned. This, of course, drastically reduces the field of our observations, but it is essential to rely on facts, which as far as possible are beyond criticism. We have included the magic of certain Australian tribes;[1] a number of Melanesian societies;[2] two Iroquois nations, the Cherokee and Huron, and the Algonquin magic of the Ojibway.[3] We have also included ancient Mexican magic;[4] the contemporary system of the Straits Settlements in Malay,[5] and two of the forms magic has assumed in India—contemporary folk magic of the north-western states and the quasi-scientific form it took under the direction of certain Brahmans of the literary period known as Vedic.[6] While we are unfortunate in the quality of material in the Semitic languages, we have not neglected this subject entirely.[7] Studies of Greek and Latin magic[8] have been particularly useful in the study of magical representations and the functioning of a well-differentiated magic. We have also used well attested material taken from the history of magic in the Middle Ages[9] and from French, Germanic, Celtic and Finnish folklore.

Notes

1 The Arunta:—B. Spencer and F. J. Gillen, *The Native Tribes of Central Australia*, London, 1898; Pitta-Pitta and neighbouring tribes in central Queensland—W. Roth, *Ethnographical Studies among the North-Western Central Queensland Aborigines*, Brisbane, 1897. G. Kurnai; Murring and neighbouring tribes of the south-east—

L. Fison and A. W. Howitt, *Kamilaroi and Kurnai*, 1885; 'On some
Australian beliefs', *Journal of the Anthropological Institute*, 1883,
xiii, p. 185 *et seq.*; 'Australian medicine-men', *J.A.I.*, xvi, p. 30
et seq. 'Notes on Australian songs and song-makers', *J.A.I.*, xvii, p. 30
et seq. These precious documents are often incomplete, particularly
as far as incantations are concerned.

2 The Banks Islands, Solomon Islands and the New Hebrides—R. H.
Codrington, *The Melanesians, their Anthropology and Folklore*,
Oxford, 1890; as well as this capital study we have used a certain
number of ethnographical works, including those of M. Gray on the
Tanna (*Proceedings of the Australian Association for the Advancement
of Science*, January 1892); cf. Sidney H. Ray, 'Some notes on the
Tannese', *Internationales Archiv für Ethnographie*, 1894, vii, p. 227
et seq. These writings are of interest since they provide information
on the subject of *mana*, but they are incomplete so far as details on
ritual, incantations and the general system of magic and the
magician are concerned.

3 Among the Cherokee we have proper texts, ritual manuscripts
written by magicians, in Sequoyah characters; J. Mooney has
collected almost 550 formulas and rituals and has often succeeded in
obtaining some of the best commentaries: *The Sacred Formulas of the
Cherokees*, 7th Annual Report of the Bureau of American Ethnology,
1891; *Myths of the Cherokee*, 19th Ann. Rep. Bur. Amer. Ethn., 1900.
For the Huron we have used only the excellent material of J. N. B.
Hewitt on the *orenda* and we give an account of them later on.
Ojibway pictograms (Algonquin), depicting initiation in diverse
magical societies have also been of great value. Both written texts
and figures are included in the work of W. J. Hoffman, *The
Mide'wiwin of the Ojibwa*, 7th Ann. Rep. Bur. Amer. Ethn., 1887.

4 For Mexican magic see the illustrated manuscripts in Spanish and
Nahuatl made for Sahagun, published, translated and commentated
by E. Seler, 'Zauberei und Zauberer im Alten Mexico', in *Veröff
a.d. Kgl. Müs. f. Völkerk.*, vii, 2, pp. 2–4, in which the material is
excellent if brief.

5 The book by W. W. Skeat, *Malay Magic*, London, 1889, contains
excellent factual reports, well analysed and complete, and observed
by the author himself or collected in a notable series of magical
manuscripts and treatises.

6 The Hindus have left us an incomparable body of magical texts:
hymns and formulas in the *Atharva Veda*, ed. R. Roth and W. D.
Whitney, 1856; edited with commentaries by Sâyana, Bombay,
1895–1900, 4 vols; translated by A. Weber, Books I–VI in *Indische
Studien*, vols 11–18; translation by V. Henry, Books VII–XIV, Paris,

Maisonneuve, 1887–96; translation with commentary and a choice of sacred songs, M. Bloomfield, 'Hymns of the Atharva-Veda', in *Sacred Books of the East*, vol. 42, Oxford, 1897; ritual texts of the *Kauçika-Sutra* (ed. Bloomfield, *J. Amer. Oriental Soc.*, 1890, xiv: partial translation with notes by W. Caland, *Altindisches Zauberritual*, Amsterdam, 1900; A. Weber, 'Omina und Portenta', in *Abhdl. d. Kgl. Ak. d. Wiss.*, Berlin, 1858, pp. 344–413). However, it should be pointed out that we are aware that these inaccurately dated texts present only a *single* Hindu tradition, a literary tradition of a *single* Brahmanical school, belonging to the Atharva-Veda. It therefore does not cover all Brahman magic, any more, of course, than it represents all the magic of ancient India. For modern India we have mainly relied on the collection by W. Crooke, *The Popular Religion and Folklore of Northern India*, 2 vols, London, 1896. It has a certain number of gaps, above all as far as details of ritual and textual formula are concerned.

7 For Assyrian magic we possess some exorcism rites only: C. Fossey, *La Magic assyrienne*, Paris 1902. We have only fragmentary material on Hebrew magic: T. W. Davies, *Magic, Divination and Demonology among the Hebrews*, Leipzig, 1898; L. Blau, *Das altjüdische Zauberwesen*, Strassburg, 1898. We have not included any discussion on Arab magic.

8 One of the authors has already provided an account of the value of Greek and Latin sources—H. Hubert, 'Magica', in *Dictionnaire des antiquités grecques et romaines*, C. V. Daremberg and E. Saglio, vi, Part 31, p. 9 *et seq.* We have preferred to rely on magical papyrus materials, which provide, if not details of whole rituals, at least exact indications of a certain number of rites. We have used the texts of alchemists (P. E. M. Berthelot, *Collection des anciens alchimistes grecs* Paris, 1887). We have used material in magical tales and stories only with great caution.

9 Our study of magic in the Middle Ages has been greatly facilitated by J. Hanson, *Zauberwahn, Inquisition und Hexenprozess im Mittelalter*, Munich, 1900, and *Quellen und Untersuchungen zur Geschichte des Hexenwahns und der Hexenverfolgung im Mittelalter*, Bonn, 1901.

chapter two

A Definition of Magic

We suggest, provisionally, that magic has been sufficiently distinguished in various societies from other systems of social facts. This being the case we have reason to believe that magic not only forms a distinct class of phenomena but that it is also susceptible to clear definition. We shall have to provide this definition for ourselves, since we cannot be content to accept facts as 'magical' simply because they have been so called by the actors themselves or observers. The points of view of such people are subjective, hence not necessarily scientific. A religion designates the remnants of former cults as 'magical' even when the rites are still being performed in a religious manner; this way of looking at things has even been followed by scholars—a folklorist as distinguished as Skeat considers the old agrarian rites of the Malays as magical. As far as we are concerned, magic should be used to refer to those things which society as a whole considers magical and not those qualified as such by a single segment of society only. However we are also aware that some societies are not very coherent in their notions of magic and, even if they are, this has only come about gradually. Consequently, we are not very optimistic about suddenly discovering an ideal definition of our subject; this must await the conclusion of our analysis of the relations between magic and religion.

In magic we have officers, actions and representations: we call a person who accomplishes magical actions a *magician*, even if he is not a professional; *magical representations* are those ideas and beliefs which correspond to magical actions; as for these actions, with regard to which we have defined the other elements of magic, we shall call them *magical rites*. At this stage it is important to distinguish between these activities and other social practices with which they might be confused.

In the first place, magic and magical rites, as a whole, are traditional facts. Actions which are never repeated cannot be called magical. If the whole community does not believe in the efficacy of a group of actions, they cannot be magical. The form of the ritual is eminently transmissible and this is sanctioned by public opinion. It follows from this that strictly individual actions, such as the private superstitions of gamblers, cannot be called magical.

The kind of traditional practices which might be confused with magical activities include legal actions, techniques and religious ritual. Magic has been linked with a system of jural obligations, since in many places there are words and gestures which are binding sanctions. It is true that legal actions may often acquire a ritual character and that contracts, oaths and trials by ordeal are to a certain extent sacramental. Nevertheless, the fact remains that although they contain ritual elements they are not magical rites in themselves. If they assume a special kind of efficacy or if they do more than merely establish contractual relations between persons, they cease to be legal actions and do become magical or religious rites. Ritual acts, on the contrary, are essentially thought to be able to produce much more than a contract: rites are eminently effective; they are creative; they *do* things. It is through these qualities that magical ritual is recognizable as such. In some cases even, ritual derives its name from a reference to these effective characteristics: in India the word which best corresponds to our word ritual is *karman*, action; sympathetic magic is the *factum, krtyâ*, par excellence. The German word *Zauber* has the same etymological meaning; in other languages the words for magic contain the root *to do*.

However, human skill can also be creative and the actions of craftsmen are known to be effective. From this point of view the greater part of the human race has always had difficulty in distinguishing techniques from rites. Moreover, there is probably not a single activity which artists and craftsmen perform which is not also believed to be within the capacity of the magician. It is because their ends are similar that they are found in natural association and constantly join forces. Nevertheless, the extent of their co-operation varies. Magic, in general, aids and abets techniques such as fishing, hunting and farming. Other arts are, in a manner of speaking, entirely swamped by magic. Medicine and alchemy are examples: for a long period technical elements were reduced to a minimum and magic became the dominant partner; they depended on magic to such an extent that they seemed to have grown from it. Medicine, almost to our own days, has remained hedged in by religious and magical taboos, prayers, incantations and astrological predictions. Furthermore, a doctor's drugs and potions and a surgeon's incisions are a real tissue of symbolic, sympathetic, homeopathic and anti-pathetic actions which are really thought of as magical. The effectiveness of the rites are not distinguished from that of the techniques; they are considered to be one and the same.

It is all the more confusing when the traditional character of magic is found to be bound up with the arts and crafts. The successive gestures of an artisan may be as uniformly regulated as those of a magician. Nevertheless, the arts and crafts have been universally distinguished from magic; there has always been an intangible difference in method between the two activities. As far as techniques are concerned, the effects are considered to be pro-duced through a person's skill. Everyone knows that the results are achieved directly through the co-ordination of action, tool and physical agent. Effect follows on immediately from cause. The results are homogeneous with the means: the javelin flies through the air because it is thrown and food is cooked by means of fire. Moreover, traditional techniques are controllable by experience which is constantly putting the value of technical beliefs to the test. The whole existence of these skills depends on a continued perception of this homogeneity between cause and effect. If an activity is both magical and technical at the same time, the magical aspect is the one which fails to live up to this definition. Thus, in medical practices, words, incantations, ritual and astrological observances are magical; this is the realm of the occult and of the spirits, a world of ideas which imbues ritual movements and gestures with a special kind of effectiveness, quite different from their mechanical effectiveness. It is not really believed that the gestures themselves bring about the result. The effect derives from some-thing else, and usually this is not of the same order. Let us take, for example, the case of a man who stirs the water of a spring in order to bring rain. This is the peculiar nature of rites which we might call *traditional actions whose effectiveness is sui generis.*

So far we have managed to define only ritual, not magical ritual, and we must now attempt to distinguish it from religious rites. Frazer, as we have seen, proposed his own criteria. The first is that magical rites are sympathetic rites. But this is not sufficient. There are not only magical rites which are not sympathetic, but neither is sympathy a prerogative of magic, since there are sympathetic practices in religion. During the festival of Succoth, when the great priest in the temple of Jerusalem poured water onto the altar, hands held high above his head, he was obviously performing a sympathetic rite destined to bring about rain. When, during a holy sacrifice, a Hindu officiant prolongs or shortens at will the life of the sacrificial victim, following the peregrination which accompanies the libation, the ritual is still eminently sympathetic. In both cases the symbolism is perfectly clear; the ritual appears to act by itself. However, in each of these rituals the dominant character is religious. The officiants, the atmosphere of the place, the presence of divinities, the gravity of the actions, the aims of the people attending the rite—all leave no doubt in our minds on this score. Sympathetic rites may therefore, be either magical or religious.

The second criterion proposed by Frazer is that a magical rite normally acts on its own, that is, constrains, while a religious rite worships and conciliates. The former has an automatic, immediate reaction; the latter acts indirectly through a kind of respectful persuasion—here the agent is a spiritual intermediary. However, this is far from satisfactory as an explanation. Religious rites may also constrain and, in most of the ancient religions, the god was unable to prevent a rite from accomplishing its end if it had been faultlessly executed. Nor is it true—as we shall see later—that all magical rites have a direct action, since spirits and even gods may be involved in magic. Finally, spirits, gods and devils do not always automatically obey the orders of a magician; the latter is often forced to supplicate to them.

We shall, therefore, have to find other criteria. To find them we shall look at the various aspects one after the other.

Among rites, there are some which are certainly religious in nature; these include ritual which is solemn, public, obligatory, regular—for example, festivals and sacraments. And yet there are rites of this kind which Frazer refused to accept as religious. As far as he was concerned, all the ceremonies of the Australian aborigines, and most of their initiation rites, are magical because of the sympathetic ritual involved. In fact, the ritual of the Arunta clans, known as the *intichiuma*—the tribal initiatory rites—have precisely that degree of importance, seriousness and holiness which the idea of religion evokes. The totemic species and ancestors present during the course of the ritual are, in fact, of the same order as those respected and feared forces, the presence of which Frazer himself takes as indicative of the religious nature of a rite. These are the very forces invoked during the ceremonies.

On the other hand, rites do exist which are consistently magical. These are the evil spells or *maléfices*, and we find them regularly qualified as such by both law and religion. The casting of evil spells is illicit and expressly prohibited and punished. This prohibition marks the formal distinction between magical and religious rites. It is the fact of prohibition itself which gives the spell its magical character. There are religious rites which are equally maleficent, such as certain cases of *devotio*, the imprecations made against a communal enemy, against persons violating tombs or breaking oaths, and all those death rites sanctioned by ritual taboos. We might go so far as to say that there are evil spells which are evil only in so far as people fear them. The fact of their being prohibited provides a delimitation for the whole sphere of magical action.

We have, in other words, two extremes which form the differing poles of magic religion: the pole of sacrifice and the pole of evil spells. Religion has always created a kind of ideal towards which people direct their hymns, vows, sacrifices, an ideal which is bolstered by prescriptions. These are areas which are avoided by magic, since association with evil as an aspect of magical rites always provides humanity with a rough general notion of magic. Between these two poles we have a confused mass of activities whose specific nature is not immediately apparent. These are practices which are neither prescribed nor proscribed in any special way. We have religious practices which are private and voluntary, as well as magical practices which are licit. On the one hand, we have the occasional actions of private cults; on the other, there are magical practices associated with technical skills, such as those of the medical profession. A European peasant who exorcizes the mice from his field, an Indian who prepares his war medicine, or a Finn who incants over his hunting weapons—they all aim at ends which are perfectly above board and perform actions which are licit. There is the same connexion between magical and domestic cults in Melanesia, where magic acts in a series of rites involving their ancestors. Far from denying the possibility of confusing magic and religion we should like to stress the fact, reserving our explanation for the situation until later. For the moment we are happy enough to accept Grimm's definition that magic is a 'kind of religion, used in the lower spheres of domestic life'. However, while the continuity between magic and religion is of great interest, we must, for the moment, begin to classify our data. In order to do this we shall enumerate a certain number of external characteristics by which they can be recognized. This inter-relationship between magic and religion has not prevented people from noting the difference between the two types of rite and hence from practising them in such a way as to show that they are aware of the difference. We must, therefore, look for these signs, which will enable us to make some kind of classification.

First of all, magical and religious rites often have different agents; in other words, they are not performed by one and the same person. By way of exception, a priest performing a magical rite does not adopt the normal comportment of his profession: he turns his back to the altar, he performs with his left hand what he usually does with his right, and so on and so forth.

There are also many other signs which should be grouped together. First there is the choice of place where the magical ceremony is to be performed. This is not generally inside a temple or at some domestic shrine. Magical rites are commonly performed in woods, far away from dwelling places, at night or in shadowy corners, in the secret recesses of a house or at any rate in some out-of-the-way place. Where religious rites are performed openly, in full public view, magical rites are carried out in secret. Even when magic is licit, it is done in secret, as if performing some maleficent deed. And even if the magician has to work in public he makes an attempt to dissemble: his gestures become furtive and his words indistinct. The medicine man and the bone-setter, working before the assembled gathering of a family, mutter their spells, cover up their actions and hide behind simulated or real ecstasies. Thus, as far as society is concerned, the magician is a being set apart and he prefers even more to retire to the depths of the forest. Among colleagues too he nearly always tries to keep himself to himself. In this way he is reserving his powers. Isolation and secrecy are two almost perfect signs of the intimate character of a magical rite. They are always features of a person or persons working in a private capacity; both the act and the actor are shrouded in mystery.

In fact, however, the various characteristics we have so far revealed only reflect the irreligiosity of magical rites. They are anti-religious and it is desired that they be so. In any case, they do not belong to those organized systems which we call cults. Religious practices, on the contrary, even fortuitous and voluntary ones, are always predictable, prescribed and official. They *do* form part of a cult. Gifts presented to gods on the occasion of a vow, or an expiatory sacrifice offered during illness, are regular kinds of homage. Although performed in each case voluntarily, they are really obligatory and inevitable actions. Magical rites, on the other hand, while they may occur regularly (as in the case of agricultural magic) and fulfil a need when they are performed for specific ends (such as a cure), are always considered unauthorized, abnormal and, at the very least, not highly estimable. Medical rites, however useful and licit they may be made to appear; do not involve the same degree of solemnity, nor the same idea of an accomplished duty, as do expiatory sacrifices or vows made to a curative divinity. When somebody has recourse to a medicine man, the owner of a spirit-fetish, a bone-mender or a magician, there is certainly a need, but no moral obligation is involved.

Nevertheless, there are examples of cults which are magical. There was the Hecate cult of Ancient Greece, the cult of Diana and the devil in the magic of the Middle Ages and the whole cult devoted to one of the greatest Hindu divinities, Rudra-Shiva. These, however, are examples of secondary developments and quite simply prove that magicians have themselves set up a cult which was modelled along the lines of religious cults.

We have thus arrived at a provisionally adequate definition of magical phenomena. A magical rite is *any rite which does not play a part in organized cults*—it is private, secret, mysterious and approaches the limit of a prohibited rite. With this definition, and taking into consideration the other elements of magic which we have mentioned, we have the first hint of its special qualities. It will be noticed that we do not define magic in terms of the structure of its rites, but by the circumstances in which these rites occur, which in turn determine the place they occupy in the totality of social customs.

chapter three

The Elements of Magic

1 The Magician

We have used the term 'magician' to apply to any practitioner of magic, whether or not he considers himself a professional. In effect, we maintain that there are magical rites which can be performed by others besides specialists. Included amongst these are 'old wives' remedies, magical medicine and all those country rites which are performed so frequently throughout the agricultural cycle; hunting and fishing rites also seem generally available to all. However, we should like to stress the fact that these rites are much less common than might appear. Moreover, they are always of a rudimentary nature and while they fulfil common needs their extent is limited. On the whole, this kind of folk magic is performed only by patres-familias or mistresses of households. And, what is more, many of these last prefer to leave the business to those more skilled or versed in the subject. The majority are wary of employing magic, whether through scruple or lack of self-confidence; there are also those who might refuse to pass on a useful remedy.

Furthermore, it would be a mistake to imagine that the amateur magician feels in his normal state when about to perform a ritual. Very often it is just because he has left his 'normal' state that he feels able to produce results. He has observed sexual abstinence; he has fasted, meditated; he has carried out certain preliminary actions; not to mention the fact that the ritual itself, at some point in time at least, turns him into another man. In addition, anyone who uses a magical formula, however trite, believes he has a proprietary right to it. The peasant who speaks of 'My grandmother's cure-all', is consequently qualified to avail himself of it; here the use of the remedy is confined to the 'métier'.

Following this train of thought, we should mention the case where all members of a society are endowed, by common belief, with qualities from birth which on occasion may become magical. This applies to the families of magicians in modern India (Ojhas in the north-western states, Baigas in Mirzapur). Members of secret societies may also acquire special magical powers through the fact of their initiation and where initiation plays an important role this may apply to the society as a whole. In short, we see that even amateur magicians, as far as their ritual practices are concerned, are not laymen pure and simple.

It is true that, though there are rites which are available to all and sundry and require little specialized skill, it is very often the case that these rites have become common knowledge through constant repetition, have become simplified through use or are commonplace by their very nature. But in all cases, there must at least be the knowledge of a remedy, the traditional approach, in order to give those who pursue the rites the minimal qualifications. Having made this observation we can now state that, as a general rule, magical practices are the prerogative of specialists. Magicians do exist, and their presence is indicated everywhere where sufficiently intensive studies have been carried out.

Not only do magicians exist, but in many societies—at least in theory—the performance of magical rites is their prerogative. This fact has been attested in the Vedic texts, where the ritual may be performed only by the *Brahman*. The person involved does not act independently, but he attends the ceremony, follows instructions passively, repeats the formulas he is told to repeat, placing his hand on the officiant during particularly solemn moments, but nothing more. In brief, he is relegated to the same role as the person who provides the sacrificial beast when the priest is performing the rite. Moreover, it appears that, as far as ancient India is concerned, the exclusive ownership of magic by magicians was not merely a theoretical rule. We have reason to believe that it was a genuine privilege possessed by the Brahmans and recognized by the *ksatriya* caste of nobles and kings. Certain scenes in Indian classical theatre provide proof of this. It is true that on all levels of society popular magic flourished, less exclusive perhaps, but even this had its practitioners. The same idea was common in Christian Europe. Whoever performed magic was reputed to be a magician and could be punished as such. The crime of magic was a common one. For the Church as for the law there could be no magic without a magician.

1 *The qualities of a magician* Nobody can become a magician at will; there are qualities which distinguish a magician from the layman. Some are acquired, some inherited; to some the qualities are lent while others actually possess them.

It is claimed that a magician can be recognized by certain physical peculiarities, with which he is branded and by which his calling may be discovered should he attempt to conceal it. It is thought, for example, that the pupils of a magician's eyes have swallowed up the iris, or that his visual images are produced back to front. He is said to lack a shadow. In the Middle Ages people looked for the devil's mark on the witch's body. Doubtless many witches were hysterical cases capable of producing stigmata and anæsthesic zones. As for the beliefs regarding the particular appearance of magicians, they mainly depend on actual observation. All over the world there are people who have a peculiarly cunning look, who appear odd or untrustworthy, who blink at one strangely. It is summed up in the idea of the 'evil eye' and applies to persons who are feared and suspected. They are all lumped together as magicians, along with nervous and jumpy individuals or subnormal peoples in those backward areas where magic still has a hold. Violent gestures, a shrill voice, oratorical or poetic gifts are often taken to be attributes of magicians. They are all signs betraying a kind of nervous condition, which in many societies may be cultivated by magicians and are manifested with greater force during ceremonies. Often they may be accompanied by nervous trances, hysterical crises, even cataleptic fits. The magician falls into a state of ecstasy, often naturally induced but more usually feigned. Then he often believes, and it seems to the onlookers, that he has been transported out of this world. From the first twitchings until his return to the world of the living, he is watched with worried attention by the spectators, who today behave similarly during hypnotic seances. These experiences deeply impress the magician, since he is prone to believe that his abnormal states are the manifestation of an unknown power which in turn makes his magic effective. These kinds of nervous phenomena, indications of spiritual gifts, qualify certain individuals to become magicians.

There are other individuals destined to become magicians who are brought to public notice by fear or suspicion, or through their physical peculiarities or extraordinary gifts—jugglers, ventriloquists and tumblers are examples. Any infirmity suffices, such as a limp, a hump or blindness. Over-sensitivity to the reactions of normal people, a persecution complex or delusions of grandeur may predispose them to believing themselves capable of special powers.

We should point out here that all these individuals—the disabled and the ecstatic, the pedlars, hawkers, jugglers and neurotics—actually form kinds of social classes. They possess magical powers not through their individual peculiarities but as a consequence of society's attitude towards them and their kind.

The same may be said of women. They are everywhere recognized as being more prone to magic than men, not so much because of their physical characteristics, but because of the social attitudes these characteristics provoke. The critical periods of their life cycle lead to bemusement and apprehension, which place them in a special position. And it is precisely at periods such as puberty, menstruation, pregnancy and childbirth that a woman's attributes reach their greatest intensity. It is usually at such times that women are supposed to provide subjects or act as agents for magical action. Old women are witches; virgins are valuable auxiliaries; menstrual blood and other like products are common specifics. Moreover, it is true that women are particularly disposed to hysteria, and their nervous crises make them susceptible to superhuman forces, which endow them with special powers. However, even outside these critical periods, which occupy a not insignificant part of their life, women are the butt of superstitions and jural and religious taboos, which clearly mark them off as a separate class in society. They are made out to be more different than men than they are in fact. They are said to be the font of mysterious activities, the sources of magical power. On the other hand, since women are excluded from most religious cults—or if admitted, reduced to a passive role—the only practices left to them on their own initiative are magical ones. The magical attributes of women derive primarily from their social position and consequently are more talked about than real. In fact, there are fewer female practitioners of magic than public opinion would have us believe. The curious result is that on the whole, it is the men who perform the magic while women are accused of it. In the *Atharva Veda* sorceresses are exorcized and all the magic is made by men. In most societies we call primitive, old women as well as younger ones are accused of crimes of witchcraft which they have never committed. In the Middle Ages, particularly from the fourth century onwards, the majority of witches were women. But here we should not forget that we are dealing with a period of persecution and our information is only derived from accounts of trials. The excessive number of witches accused then simply revealed the existence of social prejudices which the Inquisition exploited and encouraged.

Children may be in great demand as assistants to the magician, particularly in divinatory rites. Sometimes they even perform their own magical rites, as among the Australian Dieri. In modern India children draw signs in the footprints of elephants, singing the appropriate incantations. As we all know, children have a very special status; because of their age and because they have not passed through definitive initiatory rites they are still thought to possess uncertain, troublesome natures. Once again it is from being members of a particular stratum of society that they derive their magical virtues.

Magic is also part and parcel of some professions. Doctors, barbers, blacksmiths, shepherds, actors and gravediggers have magical powers, which clearly are not attributes of individuals but of corporate groups. Virtually all doctors, all shepherds and all blacksmiths are magicians: doctors because their skills go hand in hand with magic, and in any case their use of such complex techniques makes it inevitable that their profession should be considered marvellous and supernatural; barbers, because they are so intimately involved with bodily waste, which is commonly hidden away or destroyed through fear of sorcery; blacksmiths, because they work with a substance which universally provokes superstition and because their difficult profession, shrouded in mystery, is not without prestige; shepherds, because of their communion with animals, plants and stars; gravediggers, because of their contact with death. It is their profession which places these people apart from the common run of mortals, and it is this separateness which endows them with magical power. There is, of course, one profession which separates a man from his fellows more than any other— particularly as it is usually performed by a single individual on behalf of the whole society, even a large-scale society—this is the role of executioner. And we find that executioners are individuals who have access to spells and charms used for capturing thieves, trapping vampires, etc. They are magicians.

The exceptional status of those with positions of authority in society also makes a magician. Among the Australian Arunta, the chief of the local totemic group, its master of ceremonies, is at the same time a sorcerer. In New Guinea most influential members of society are magicians; there are grounds for believing that throughout Melanesia, the chief—an individual who possesses *mana*, that is, spiritual force—is endowed with magical as well as religious powers. It is no doubt for the same reasons that the mythical princes in the epic poetry of the Hindus and Celts were said to possess magical attributes. These facts are sufficiently important for Frazer to have introduced the study of magic into his work on divine priest-kings although, as far as we are concerned, kings are more godly and priestly than they are magical. On the other hand magicians may possess political authority of the first order. They can be highly influential, often important personages. Thus the social status predestines certain individuals to the exercise of magical power and vice versa the practice of magic ordains their social status.

In societies where sacred functions are completely specialized, priests are often suspected of magic. In the Middle Ages priests were considered to be liable to attack from demons and as a result were tempted to indulge in demoniacal—that is, magical—activities themselves. In such cases, it was their role as priest which led to their being considered magicians. Their celibacy, their life of isolation and as consecrated officers of the church in constant touch with the supernatural, all help to set them apart from others and expose them to suspicion. Such suspicions appear to have often been justified. The priest either devotes himself to magic for his own sake, or his participation is considered essential for the carrying out of magical ceremonies and he is forced to play his part in them, often indeed without knowing it. Wicked priests, particularly those who have broken their vows of chastity, are naturally more exposed to accusations of magic.

Once a church loses its following the members of the new religion consider the former priests to be magicians. The Malays or the Moslem Shams treat the *pawang* and the *paja* as magicians; in fact, they were former priests. Heresy also leads to acts of magic: the Catharists and the Vaudois were considered to be sorcerers. However, as in Catholicism the idea of magic covers the notion of a false religion and since this is a different phenomenon, we shall keep it for later study. The situation is, nevertheless, of interest here, since magic is once again seen to be attributed to a whole group. Up till now, we have found that magicians have been recruited from classes which have only a secondary interest in magic. Here on the contrary members of a religious sect are considered to be magicians. All Jews were magicians in the eyes of the Alexandrians, for example, as well as for the mediæval church.

In the same way, strangers in a community are grouped as sorcerers. In some Australian tribes all natural deaths which occurred within the group were accredited to the witchcraft of a neighbouring group and resulted in vendettas and feuding. The two villages of Toaripi and Koitapu at Port Moresby in New Guinea spent their time (according to Chalmers) accusing each other of witchcraft. This situation is well-nigh universal amongst primitive peoples. Indeed one of the names given to the sorcerers in Vedic India was that of 'stranger'. A stranger is pre-eminently someone living on foreign territory—the hostile neighbour. One might say, accepting this viewpoint, that magical powers are delimited topographically. We have an example of just such a precise delimitation of magic in an Assyrian exorcization rite: 'Witch, you are bewitched, I am free; Elamite witch, I am free; Qutean witch, I am free; Sutean witch, I am free; Lullubian witch, I am free; Shannigalbian witch, I am free.' (K. N. Tallqvist, *Die Assyrische Beschwörungsserie Maglü*, iv, pp. 99–103.) When two cultures come into contact, magic is usually attributed to the lesser developed. Classic examples are the Dasyus of India, and the Finns and the Lapps, accused respectively of sorcery by the Hindus and the Scandinavians. All forest dwellers in Melanesia and Africa are sorcerers in the eyes of the more advanced tribes of the plains, the coast and rivers. Nomadic tribes living amongst a sedentary people are also thought to be sorcerers. This is the case even today with gypsies and the numerous wandering Indian caste groups—traders, leatherworkers and blacksmiths. And within these extraneous groups, certain clans or families are more gifted in the art of magic than others.

It would seem that these accusations of magic are not always unjustified. Some groups, in fact, claim to possess superhuman powers over certain phenomena, in some cases religious, in others magical. As far as the Greeks, Arabs and Jesuits were concerned the Brahmans were real magicians and were actually attributed with quasi-divine powers. There are groups who claim to be able to produce or withhold the wind or rain and who are recognized by their neighbours as possessing these gifts. In an Australian tribe in Mount Gambier there is a clan which 'owns the wind'. They are accused by their neighbours, the Booandik, of producing rain and wind at will. Even the Lapps sold sacks full of wind to European sailors.

We conclude then that, since certain persons dedicate themselves to magic as a result of the social attitudes attached to their status, magicians (who do not belong to a special class), must equally be the object of strong social feelings and that these feelings, which are directed towards magicians who are nothing but magicians, are of the same nature as those existing where it has been thought that among all the classes previously considered, there were magical powers. And, since these feelings are provoked principally by their abnormal character, we can conclude that a magician has, in so far as he has one, a social status which may be defined as abnormal. However, we do not wish to stress the negative side of the magician's role and would rather turn to a study of his positive qualities and his particular gifts.

We have already pointed to certain positive characteristics which incline a person to the role of magician: a nervous disposition, skill, etc. Magicians are usually thought to have wonderful dexterity and an outstanding knowledge. A simplistic theory of magic might speculate on their intelligence and the marvels they perform, and explain their profession as a complete tissue of inventions and hoaxes. Yet these concrete characteristics which continue to be attributed hypothetically to the magician form only one part of his traditional image; many other features have also served to bolster his prestige.

Included among these are those mythical and fantastical elements which feature in myths, or rather in a society's oral traditions which are generally recounted in the form of legends, fairy tales or romances. These traditions hold a considerable place in the folk cultures of the world and form an important part of the study of folklore. As the famous Somadeva collection of Hindu tales says: 'The gods live in a constant state of happiness, and men in perpetual distress; the actions of those who mediate between men and gods, through the diversity of their lot, are always acceptable and entertaining. For this reason I shall tell you the story of the life of the Vidyâdhâras', that is, the demons and consequently the magicians (*Kathâ-Sâra-Sârit-Sagara*, I, 1, 47). These legends and tales are not simply exercises of the imagination or a traditional expression of collective fantasies, but their constant repetition, during the course of long evening sessions, bring about a note of expectation, of fear, which at the slightest encouragement may induce illusions and provoke the liveliest reactions. Moreover, in these cases there is no possible boundary between fable and belief, between legend on the one hand and real history and myths automatically believed on the other. People listen to a magician talking and watch him at work and they also consult him. They attribute to him such great powers that no one can doubt his ability easily to succeed in executing those little services which are required of him. How is it possible *not* to believe that a Brahman—a being superior to the gods themselves, a being who can create a whole universe—could not, at least from time to time, cure a cow? The image of the magician grows from story to story, and from teller to teller, precisely because he is a favourite hero of folk imagination; either because the people have their own personal problems or because of the picturesque interest which magic automatically excites. The powers of a priest are determined once and for all by the religious dogma, but the image of the magicians is created outside magic. It is created by an infinity of 'once upon a times', and all the magician has to do is to live up to this portrait. We should not be surprised, therefore, if the literary traits of the heroes of our magical stories are also typical characteristics of the real magician.

The mythical qualities of which we have been speaking are powers or produce power. What appeals most to the imagination is the ease with which the magician achieves his ends. He has the gift of conjuring up more things than any ordinary mortals can dream of. His words, his gestures, his glances, even his thoughts are forces in themselves. His own person emanates influences before which nature and men, spirits and gods must give way.

Apart from a general power over objects, the magician has power over his own being and this is the prime source of his strength. Through force of will he accomplishes things beyond the power of normal human beings. The laws of gravity do not apply to the magician. He is an expert at levitation and can betake himself anywhere he wishes in a trice. He is to be found in many places at once. Even the laws of contradiction do not apply to him. In 1221 Johannes Teutonicus of Halberstadt, a preacher and sorcerer, is said to have performed three masses, concurrently, at Halberstadt, Mainz and Cologne. Tales of this kind are plentiful. In the minds of believers in magic the exact nature of the magician's locomotion remains essentially uncertain. Is it the individual himself, his own person, which moves? Or is it his double or his soul which goes in his place? Only theologians and philosophers have attempted to solve this paradox. The ordinary man does not care a fig. Magicians have taken advantage of this uncertainty, encouraging it as another aspect of the mystery which surrounds their activities. We ourselves have no intention of trying to solve these contradictions; they arise from a basic vagueness of primitive thinking concerning the idea of the soul and the idea of the body. This vagueness is a more important factor than is normally believed.

Of these two concepts only that of the soul lends itself to sufficient elaboration, thanks to the mystery and wonder it conjures up in our minds even to this day. A magician's soul is an astonishing thing. It has even more fantastic, more occult qualities, much darker depths, than the run of human souls. A magician's soul is essentially mobile, easily separated from his body. When primitive forms of animist belief fade away and people cease to believe a mortal's soul wanders around while he dreams, or can be changed into a fly or a butterfly, it still happens that the old beliefs are applied to the magician. They may even provide a means of recognizing him, for example when one is found asleep with a fly circling around his mouth. At all events, unlike ordinary souls whose movements are involuntary, a magician may send out his soul at will. Among the Australian Kurnai, during a spirit seance, the 'barn' sends out his soul to spy on advancing enemies. In India we also have the case of the Yogins, although their mystical theology is really more philosophical than religious, and more religious than magical. In applying themselves to a task (verb *yuj*), they are joining (verb *yuj*) with the primary transcendental principle of the world, a union which produces (verb *sidh*) magical power (*siddhi*). The *sutras* of Pâtanjali are explicit on this point and even attribute the capacity to other magicians beside the Yogins. The commentaries of the *Sutra*, iv, I, reveal that the *siddhi* principle involves levitation. In general, any individual who has the power to send forth his soul is a magician. We have come across no exceptions to this rule. It is the basic principle behind the whole institution designated by the poorly chosen name of *shamanism*.

A soul is a person's double, that is, it is not an anonymous part of his person, but the person himself. It is transported at will to any place and its activities there are physical ones. In some cases even, the magician is said to split himself in two. Thus the Dayak sorcerer departs to seek his medicines while he is attending a spiritualistic seance. The people see the magician's body yet he is both spiritually and corporeally absent since his double is not merely pure spirit. The two parts of the double are identical to the point that they are strictly interchangeable, one for the other. In fact it would not be far fetched to imagine the magician splitting himself in two in this way, leaving his double on the spot and taking his real self off somewhere else. This is how the flights of mediæval magicians were explained. It was said that the magician attended the sabbaths, leaving a demon in his bed, a *vicarium daemonem*. This demon counterpart was in fact his double. This example shows that the same idea of splitting oneself in two may have quite opposite results. Moreover, this basic power of the magician may be conceived in a thousand different ways involving an infinity of degrees.

A magician's double may be a fleeting materialization of his breath and his spell—a whirlwind or a dustcloud, out of which on occasion, appears the corporeal figure of his soul or even himself. On other occasions the double may be quite separate from the magician, a person to some degree independent of his control, who from time to time appears to carry out his will. The magician may be escorted by a retinue of assistants, animals or spirits, who are none other than his doubles or external souls.

Midway between these two extremes we have shape-changing. This is, in fact, a kind of splitting in two which involves animal disguises, and while the metamorphosis seems to involve two formal beings, they are, in essence, still one. Perhaps the most common examples of this kind of shape-changing occur when one of the forms seems to cancel out the other. It was through shape-changing that European witches were supposed to have indulged in aerial flights. These two themes became so intimately connected that they merged into one and the same idea. In the Middle Ages, we had the *striga*, an idea stemming originally from Greco-Roman antiquity; the *striga*, the old *strix*, is both a witch and a bird. The female witch can be seen outside her dwelling in the form of a black cat, a hare, or she-wolf, while a warlock is a goat, etc. When they are bent on doing evil, they do as animals, and if discovered they are said to be found in their animal shape. Nevertheless, even then a relative independence is always maintained between the two images. On the one hand, a sorcerer keeps his human shape during night flights, simply by climbing onto the back of his erstwhile animal form. On the other hand, it can happen that continuity is broken, the sorcerer and his animal double sometimes being found engaged in different activities at the same time. In this case, the animal is no longer a witch's counterpart; it is her familiar and the witch remains quite separate. This was the case with the cat Rutterkin which belonged to the witches Margaret and Filippa Flower, who were burnt at Lincoln on 11 March 1619 for bewitching a kinsman of the Duke of Rutland. At all events, in all cases of complete metamorphosis, the ubiquity of the magician is an undoubted fact. We can never know when coming across a witch's animal shape whether we are dealing with the witch herself or a mere deputy. There is no way out of this confusion inherent in primitive thinking, which we mentioned earlier.

The metamorphosis among European witches does not involve indiscriminate shape-changing. They usually stick to one animal— a mare, a frog, a cat, etc. These facts lead us to suppose that shape-changing involves a regular association with a single species of animal. One comes across these kinds of associations throughout the world. Algonquin, Iroquois and Cherokee medicine men—and probably all American Indian medicine men—possess manitous in order to speak Ojibway. In certain Melanesian islands magicians own snakes and sharks which act as their servants. In all these cases it is the rule that the magician's powers derive from his dealings with animals. He obtains power from his animal associates who impart to him magical formulas and ritual. On occasion the limits of his powers may even be determined by this alliance. Among the Red Indians the magician's animal auxiliary gives him control over all beasts of his species and over all things related to this species. It is in this sense that Jamblique spoke of μάγοι λεόντων and μάγοι ὄφεων who had power over lions and snakes respectively and could heal wounds inflicted by them.

In the main, apart from a few very rare cases, it is not a particular animal, but a whole species of animal with whom the magician has a relationship. Here there is a resemblance with totemic relationships. Are they in fact totemic? Our conjectures for the European situation have been shown to be true for Australia and North America, where the animal involved is really a totem being. A. W. Howitt tells the story of a Murring sorcerer who was carried off to the land of the kangaroos. As a result, the kangaroo became his totem and he could no longer partake of this animal's flesh. It may be true that magicians are the first, and also the last, to enjoy revelations of this kind and as a result are provided with individual totems. It is even plausible that, during the decline of totemism, it was primarily magician families who inherited clan totems and continued the old traditions. This is true of the Melanesian family group—known as the Octopus—who had the power to ensure successful catches of this creature. If we were able to demonstrate with any certainty that all magical relations with animals had a totemic origin we might conclude that in relationships of this kind the magician is qualified in his art through totemic affinities. At this stage all we can do is to conclude that we are dealing, not with fantasy, but with a series of facts showing examples of actual social conventions, which help us to determine the magician's status. It would be a mistake to quarrel with this interpretation by pointing out that some societies lack totemism altogether—Brahman India might be a case in point. For one thing, we know Brahman magic only from literary texts of rituals, which are the works of experts in magic and are far from the primitive roots; for another, the theme of shape-changing is not entirely absent from India as a whole and there are tales and Jâtakas galore which abound with demons, saints and magicians who change their shape. Folklore and Hindu magical custom are living proof of this tradition.

We have already mentioned witches' familiars. It is difficult to distinguish these from those animals with whom magicians have a totemic kinship or some other kind of relationship. They are, or can be considered to be, spirits. As for the spirits they usually have animal forms, either real or fantastic. Moreover, the twin themes of animal familiars and spirit auxiliaries share the notion that the magician derives his power from a source external to himself. His magical skills derive from an association with partners who maintain a certain independence. As with the separating of the magician's soul from his body, this association varies in degree and form. It may be quite tenuous, consisting merely of the simple power of occasionally communing with the spirits. The magician knows where they dwell, knows their language and through ritual is able to contact them. These are usually the kinds of relationship a person has with the dead, with fairies and other spirits of this kind (the *Hantus* of the Malays, the *Iruntarinias* of the Arunta, the Hindu *Devatâs*, etc.). In several of the Melanesian islands the magician usually derives his power from the souls of his dead kinsfolk.

Kinship is a common factor in the relations between a magician and the spirits. He is said to have a father, a mother or an ancestor who is a spirit being. In India today a certain number of families claim that their magical gifts originated this way. In Wales, families who monopolize the so-called magical arts are said to be descended from the union of a man and a fairy. More commonly, however, the relationship between a magician and a spirit is described as a kind of contract or pact, either tacit or expressed, general or particular, permanent or temporary. Here we have a kind of legal tie binding the two parties. In the Middle Ages these pacts were written deeds, sealed by blood with which it was written or signed. They were in fact blood pacts. In fairy tales these contracts appear in less solemn form—as a wager, a race or an ordeal—in which the spirit, the demon or the devil usually loses the contest.

People often like to envisage these relations under a sexual guise: witches have incubi and women who have nightmares about incubi are considered to be witches. This situation is found in places as far apart as Europe and New Caledonia, and no doubt elsewhere. The European sabbath inevitably conjures up images of sexual escapades involving witches and devils. These relations may even result in marriage or a permanent contract. It is the kind of relationship which is far from being a subsidiary feature of magic. In the Middle Ages and also in Greco-Roman times they helped provide a positive picture of the magician. The witch has always been considered a lascivious creature, a kind of courtesan, and it was as a result of the controversy engendered by the *concubitus daemonum* which shed a good deal of light on the nature of magic. The many different ways of expressing the relationship between a demon and a magician may be found together. For example, there is the story of a Rajput who, having made a female glanders' spirit his prisoner, took her to his home and to this day it is thought that the descendants of the couple have an hereditary power over the wind. It is possible to see in this example the themes of play, pact and kinship at the same time.

These relations are not externally or incidentally conceived, but profoundly affect the physical and moral condition of the magician. He bears the mark of his ally, the devil. Australian sorcerers have holes made in their tongues by the spirits; their stomachs may have been opened up and their entrails refurbished, so to speak. In the Banks Islands some sorcerers have their tongues pierced by a green snake (maé). The magician usually is capable of being possessed, like the wizard—a fact which rarely applies to the priest. Moreover, he is conscious of it and generally knows the spirit who possesses him. Belief in possessed witches is universal. In Christian Europe the belief was so widely held that witches were exorcized. Conversely, possessed persons are generally considered to be witches. And not only are the powers and status of a magician explained through the fact of his being possessed; in many cases of magical systems, possession plays the fundamental role in all magical activities. Shamanism in Siberia and Malaysia is universal. When the sorcerer is possessed he not only feels the presence of a new person within him, but his own personality succumbs to the power of the demon, and it is this spirit which speaks words through his mouth. Excluding the many cases of feigned possession—which anyway imitate the real state—we find that we are dealing with psychological and physiological states, involving the splitting of a person's personality. It is a remarkable fact that a magician, to a certain extent, can control his possession; he brings it on by appropriate practices, such as dancing, monotonous music or intoxication. To sum up, one of the magician's professional qualifications, which is not only mythical but practical, is the power of being possessed and it is a skill at which they have long been expert. From both the individual's and society's point of view, sending out a soul or receiving one are two ways of looking at the same phenomena. In the case of the individual, his personality undergoes a change; as far as society is concerned the magician is being carried off into the world of spirits. These two types of representation may sometimes coincide: the Sioux or Ojibway shaman who performs only when possessed, acquires his animal manitou only during excursions of the soul.

All myths about magicians have certain features in common. We should not have had to dwell on them at such length if they did not provide hints concerning society's opinion about magicians. A magician is seen in terms of his relationship with animals as well as his relationship with spirits, and in the last analysis he is seen in terms of his own soul. The liaison between a magician and his spirit often develops into a complete identity one with the other. This is, of course easier if the magician and the magic spirit bear the same name, and this is so frequent it almost amounts to a rule. Generally there is no need to distinguish one from the other. In this way we can see to what extent magicians exist outside the norm. This is particularly so when their souls have left their bodies, that is to say when they are performing. Thus, as we said earlier, they really belong more to the world of the spirits than to the world of men.

Thus, if a man does not qualify as a magician through his social status, he may nevertheless do so because of the coherent representations which are directed at him. A magician is a man who has special qualifications—special relationships and, more particularly, special powers. It is one of the highest classed professions and probably one of the first to be so. It is so bound up with social qualifications that individuals cannot simply join independently of their own accord. And there have been many examples of magicians who were forced, in spite of themselves, to join the fraternity.

It is public opinion which makes the magician and creates the power he wields. Thanks to public opinion he knows everything and can do anything. If nature holds no secrets from him, if he draws his powers from the primary sources of light, from the sun, the planets, the rainbow or the depths of all water, it is public opinion which desires that he should. Moreover, society does not always credit all magicians with unlimited powers or, indeed, the same powers. For the most part, even in closely knit units of society, magicians possess varied powers. Not only is the magician's profession a specialized one, but the profession itself has its own specialized features and functions.

2 *Initiation, magic in society* By what process does public opinion accept a person as a magician and how does he himself achieve this status? Individuals become magicians through revelation, through consecration and through tradition. This threefold process of qualification has been pointed out by observers and magicians alike, and very often results in distinguishing different categories of sorcerers. The *Sutra* of Patanjali mentioned previously (iv, I) says that '*siddhi* (magical powers) derive from birth, from plants, formulas, from ascetic fervour and ecstasy'.

Revelation occurs whenever a man believes himself to be in contact with one or more spirits, who place themselves at his service and teach him doctrine. This kind of initiation provides the theme of many myths and tales which can be either very simple or very complex. The simple type includes variations on the theme of

Mephistopheles and Faust; but there are others which are very elaborate. Among the Murring, the would-be sorcerer (*murup*, spirit) sleeps on the grave of an old woman. He has to cut away the skin of her stomach and while he is sleeping the skin, that is the *murup*, of the old woman, transports him beyond the vault of the sky where he meets the spirits and the gods who pass on to him secret rites and formulas. When he wakes he finds that his body has been stuffed full of pieces of quartz, like a medicine bag. During rites later, he removes them from his mouth as gifts and tokens received from the spirit world. In this case, the magician travels to the world of the spirits. In others, it is the spirit who comes to seek out the magician, and revelation is thus achieved through possession, as among the Sioux and Malays. In both these cases, the magician obtains advantages of a permanent nature through momentary contact with the spirits. To obtain the permanence of this magical transformation, it is said that the magician's personality has been profoundly modified, as we have already described. The spirits have refashioned his entrails, beaten him with their weapons, bitten him on the tongue—among the central Australian tribes the hole in his tongue is proof of the treatment meted out to the magician. It is expressly stated that the novice actually dies in order to be reborn after his revelation.

The idea of a temporary death is a common theme in both magical and religious initiations. But magicians depend more on the tales of these resurrections than others do. To diverge a moment from our set field of study, we shall mention a tale of the Baffin Land Eskimoes. A man who wished to become an *angekok* was killed by the initiating *angekok* expert. For a week he remained in a frozen state during which time his soul wandered through the ocean deeps, far into the bowels of the earth and high into the sky, learning nature's secrets. When the *angekok* woke him up again—blowing on each of his limbs—he had become an *angekok* himself. Here we have a picture of a complete revelation, in several stages, including personal revelation, travelling in the world of the spirits, learning the science of magic—in sum, acquiring knowledge of the universe.

Magical powers are obtained through the separation of the soul from the body. In the case of the shaman, however, separation and possession must be constantly repeated. For the magician these initiatory separations need occur only once in his lifetime and provide him with permanent advantages. However, they are necessary, even obligatory, at least once. In fact, the mythical representations really parallel the actual initiatory ceremonies. The individual goes to sleep in the forest on a grave, carries out a series of tasks, gives himself up to ascetic practices, deprivations and taboos, which are rites in themselves. In addition, the individual falls into a state of ecstasy and has visions, which are not purely imaginary even when the magician initiates them himself.

But it is more common for other magicians to take part. Among the *Shames* an old paja induces the initiates' first ecstasies. Moreover, it usually happens that the novice is put through an actual ordination rite, with practising magicians in charge of the ceremony. The Arunta, as well as practising initiation by spirits, also undergo initiations by magicians, with ascetic rituals, frictions, unctions and a whole series of ceremonies, during the course of which the novice absorbs small pebbles (symbols of magical power) which come from his sponsor. In the Greek manuscripts we possess a lengthy handbook on magical ordinations, the ὀγδόη Μωϋσέως (Dietrich, *Abraxus*, p. 116 *et seq*.), which reveals in detail every stage of similar ceremonies involving purification, sacrificial ritual, invocation and, to crown all, a mythical revelation explaining the secrets of the universe. So complex a ritual is not always essential. Ordination may be achieved through a communal evocation of the spirits (which is what happens in the case of the Straits Malay *pawang*) or a simple presentation of the novice to the spirits in a holy place (as in Melanesia, for example). At all events, magical initiation produces the same results as other types of initiation: it causes a change in the personality, which may sometimes be expressed, if so desired, by a change of name. Once and for all an intimate relationship is set up between an individual and his supernatural allies, a kind of permanent possession. In some societies magical initiation often merges in with religious initiation. The Red Indian Iroquois or Sioux acquire their medicines the moment they become members of the secret society. We hazard the conjecture—although there is no absolute proof—that the same applies in some Melanesian societies.

When initiatory rites become simplified, they end up resembling traditional lore, pure and simple. Magical lore, however, has never been anything quite so simple or banal. In fact, when the teacher communicates his formulas, he and the novice as well as the members of his entourage—if there are any—strike extraordinary

attitudes. The adept is said to be—and he himself believes it—one
of the elect. It is all very solemn and the mystery associated with it
does not detract from the solemnity. It is accompanied by rites and
lustrations, and hedged in by taboos; the time and place are chosen
with care. In some cases the transmission of very serious details of
magical lore is preceded by a kind of cosmological revelation on
which it appears to depend. Often magical secrets are imparted only
under certain conditions. Even a person who has bought a charm
cannot dispose of it at will outside the contract. A charm which is
transferred improperly to another person loses any powers it had or
reacts on the person who has it. Folklore all over the world provides
an infinite number of such examples. In these practices we have
hints of a state of mind which exists each time magical knowledge is
transmitted from one person to another, even magic of the most
common kind. The way this kind of lore—this pact—is transmitted
shows that even if the secrets do pass from hand to hand, the
knowledge is really the prerogative of a closed group. Revelation,
initiation and the handing down of traditional lore are, from this
point of view, equivalent. Each in its own way marks the fact that a
new member has joined the magician's association.

It is not only public opinion which considers magicians to be a
class apart; they believe it themselves as well. Although they are
outsiders, as we pointed out earlier, they also form magical cor-
porations recruited through heredity or through voluntary member-
ship. Greek writers mention families of magicians and they were
also found in Celtic countries, in India, Malaysia and Melanesia.
Magic is a kind of wealth which is carefully kept in the family. It
need not necessarily be passed down the same line as other kinds of
property. In parts of Melanesia, where matriliny is the rule, magic
is inherited from father to son; in Wales it seems that mothers
handed it down to sons, while fathers bequeathed it to the daughters.
In societies where voluntary secret societies for men play an important role, the association of magicians and the secret society usually
overlap. The magicians' associations mentioned in the Greek
parchments parallel similar mystical Alexandrine societies. On the
whole, where there are groups of magicians it is difficult to distinguish them from religious groups. It is clear that in the Middle
Ages, magic was always seen as the work of fraternities. Our
earliest texts mention witch covens and we find the same thing in
the myth of the cavalcade which followed Diana, and then in the

D

sabbath. This is clearly an exaggerated view, despite the fact that magical sects and witchcraft epidemics are well attested. Yet, while we must take exaggerated public opinion and myth into account when studying these families and sects of magicians, there is sufficient evidence to show that magic must always have functioned, at least partly, in small groups of the kind which today are formed by believers in the occult. Moreover, even when there is no formal grouping of magicians, we have in fact a professional class and this class has rules which are obeyed implicitly. We find that magicians usually follow a set of rules, which is a corporate discipline. These rules sometimes consist of a search for moral virtues and ritual purity, sometimes of a certain solemnity in their comportment, and also in other ways. The point is that they are professionals who deck themselves out with the trappings of a profession.

There may be people who will object to what we have been saying about the social character of these practitioners of magic by saying there is a folk magic which exists and is not performed by qualified persons; we can only reply that here the agents always try to resemble, as far as possible, their idea of a magician. Moreover, we should point out that this folk magic exists only in the form of survivals, in very simple little communities, hamlets or families. And we could maintain, not without some semblance of reason, that these small communities, whose members vaguely reproduce the same magical gestures of their forebears, are well and truly associations of magicians.

2 The Actions

The actions of a magician are rites. In describing them we shall demonstrate how well they correspond to our whole concept of ritual. We should point out that in collections of folklore they are often presented in forms which seem very uncomplicated, very commonplace. If the folklorists had not informed us that they were, in fact, rites, we should be inclined to consider them as everyday gestures, entirely lacking any special character. Their apparent simplicity, however, is a result of their being poorly described or poorly observed; or else they are shadows of their former selves. We shall obviously avoid those poorly described, limited rituals in our search for the typical features of magical rites.

Fortunately we possess descriptions of a great number of rites which are very complex indeed. Hindu sympathetic rites, for example, are extraordinarily intricate (*Kaucika sûtra*, 47–9). A whole range of wooden materials of ill-omen are required, along with herbs chopped in special ways, special kinds of oil, pieces of charred wood. People face a different direction from that adopted in rites of good fortune. The ritual is performed in a lonely place where the land is waste on special days—described in esoteric terms and clearly referring to evil auguries—and in shady spots (*aroka*), under an evil asterism. Then comes the special initiation rite, a long one, for the person involved—a *dîskâ*, according to the commentary (Kecava ad *sû* 12), similar to the initiation undergone in holy sacrifices. It is the Brahman, at this point, who becomes the protagonist of the main rite, or rather rites, which constitute the sympathetic magic proper. It is impossible to judge from the texts whether the thirty-two types of rites we have counted (47, 23 to 49, 27), many of which have as many as three forms, are merely part of one huge ceremony or whether they are theoretically distinct one from the other. Nevertheless, even the least complicated of them, performed in a mud shelter (49, 23), lasts no fewer than twelve days. The magic finishes with a ritual purification (49, 27). Imprecatory ritual among the Cherokee and the Pitta-Pitta in Queensland are hardly simpler. Finally, our Greek parchments and Assyrian texts give rituals of exorcization and divination which are no less elaborate.

1 *The conditions of the rites*   In beginning an analysis of rites in general, we should first point out that magical precepts not only include one or more central operations, but also enumerate a certain number of dependent observances, which are exactly akin to those which accompany religious ritual. Every time we come across genuine rituals or liturgical manuals, a precise enumeration of these circumstantial details is always included.

The time and place of the ritual are strictly prescribed. Some ceremonies may take place only at night, or at special hours of the night—at midnight, for example. Others occur at special times in the day, at sunset or sunrise—two periods which are specially magical. The day of the week is also laid down: Friday, for example, is the witches' sabbath, although without prejudice to other days. As soon as the notion of a regular week exists, rites take place on particular days. Similarly, special periods of the month are favourable, and probably almost always depend on the waxing and waning of the moon. Lunar dates are the ones most commonly fixed for the times of observance. In ancient India all magical rites theoretically involved sacrifices to the new moon or the full moon. It seems from older texts and also from modern descriptions that the brighter half of the month was reserved for rites of good omen, while the darker dates were devoted to those of evil omen. The course of the astral bodies, the conjunctions and oppositions of the moon, the sun and the planets, the positions of the stars, are all taken into consideration. It was in this way that astrology became part and parcel of magic. Some of our Greek magical texts are even found in works of astrology, and in India, in the astrological-astronomical texts of the later Middle Ages, the whole of the latter section is devoted to magic. The month and the order of the year in a general cycle are also sometimes taken into consideration. Solstitial and equinoctial days and particularly their eves, intercalary days, great festivals—of the Christian saints, for example—are all periods which are held to be special and exceptionally propitious. Of course, it sometimes happens that all these rules and regulations become so hopelessly entangled that perfect conditions can very rarely be realized. If the Hindu magicians are to be believed, some of their rights could be practised successfully only once every forty-five years.

Magic is not performed just anywhere, but in specially qualified places. Magic as well as religion has genuine sanctuaries. There are cases where such sanctuaries are used for both purposes, in Melanesia and Malaysia, for example. In modern India the altar of the village deity is also used for magical purposes and in Christian Europe some magical rites must perforce be performed in church, even on the altar. In other cases sites are chosen specifically because religious rites cannot be performed there—because they are impure, or in some way considered special. Cemeteries, crossroads, woods, marshes, rubbish heaps—are all places where ghosts and demons may be found and are highly favoured for the performance of magic. Ceremonies are also carried out on the boundaries of village and field, on thresholds, hearths, rooftops, on central beams, streets, roads or paths, in any place, in fact, which has some specific use. A minimal qualification in these cases requires that the spot has some correlation with the object of the rite. In order to harm an enemy they spit towards his house or at his feet. If the spot has no special characteristic the magician may draw a magical circle or square, a *templum*, around him and he performs his magic inside this.

It is clear, therefore, that magic, along with sacrifice, has provision for determining the time and place of ritual. There are other provisions. During ritual, materials and tools are employed which are not just everyday things. Their choice and preparation are made ritually and they are themselves also subject to special conditions of time and place. The Cherokee shaman goes off herb-hunting at a certain day of the moon, always at daybreak; he collects the herbs in a particular order, picking them with particular fingers, being careful not to let his shadow fall on the leaves and performing ritual peregrinations beforehand. Lead is taken from a bath, earth from a cemetery and so on. The confection or preparation of these materials, the ritual ingredients, is a long and finicking business. In India everything that goes into an amulet or a philtre is first of all chewed, and rubbed a long time in advance and in a strictly prescribed fashion. Magical objects, while they may not be consecrated in a religious sense, are at least medicated, and this provides them with a kind of magical consecration.

Apart from such preliminary consecration, most materials used qualify for the ritual by their innate qualities—like some sacrificial victim. Some derive these qualities from religion—they are the remains of a sacrifice which should have been consumed or destroyed—the bones of the dead, water used in lustrations, etc. Others may have features which should, in a manner of speaking, disqualify them—they are left-overs from meals, filth, nail-parings, hair-leavings, excrement, foetuses, household detritus—on the whole anything which is usually thrown away or considered useless. There is also a certain class of objects which appear to be used for their own sakes by virtue of their real or imagined properties, or again because they coincide with the nature of the rite: special animals, plants or stones. Finally, there are other types of substances such as wax, glue, plaster, water, honey, milk, used to bind the mixture or serve as a base for others and constitute, as it were, the plate on which the magic cuisine is served up. These substances themselves have special properties and may be the object of taboos which are sometimes very formal. In India it is usually laid down that the milk used should come from a cow of a particular hue, which also has a calf of identical colour. These are the materials which together comprise our magical pharmacopoeia; in learning magic their enumeration is given the same vital emphasis as the learning of religious dogmas. In the Greco-Roman world the substances used are so innumerable as to appear almost endless, yet we possess no magical ritual or practical codes for the Greco-Roman period which are at all general or complete. We do not doubt that for any single group of magicians, at any one period, the materials must normally have been prescribed in the same way as they are in the Atharvanic texts, in chapters 8 to 11 of the *Kaucika Sutra*, and even in the Cherokee texts. The list of ingredients, at least to our way of thinking, always had the imperative character of a pharmaceutical codex. We hold that those texts of magical pharmacopoeia which have come down to us complete are—each in its own time—comprehensive and limitative handbooks for a magician or a circle of magicians.

Apart from the materials, we also have the tools of the magician, which themselves always ended up having their own magical qualities. The simplest of these instruments is the magic wand, while the Chinese divining compass was perhaps one of the more complex. Greco-Latin magicians had a veritable arsenal of bowls, rings, knives, ladders, discs, rattles, bobbins, keys, mirrors, etc. The medicine bag of an Iroquois or a Sioux Indian, with its dolls, feathers, pebbles, woven beads, bones, praying sticks, knives and arrows, is as full of heterogeneous bits and pieces as the cabinet of Dr Faustus.

When we come to the roles of the magician and his client, in relation to magical ritual, we find they play the same role as the priest and the worshipper in relation to sacrifice. They also undergo preliminary rites which involve the individuals alone, their whole families or even the entire community. Among many prescriptions, they must remain chaste and pure, washing and annointing their bodies prior to the rite; they may have to fast or abstain from certain foods; they are told to wear special clothes, either brand-new or worn, pure white or with purple bands, etc; they wear make-up, masks, disguise themselves, put on special headgear, etc: sometimes they are naked, either in order to remove all barriers between them and magical forces or perhaps in order to act through ritual impropriety like the good lady of the fables. Finally special mental states are also demanded—you must have faith, the whole thing must be treated with the utmost seriousness.

All these observations concerning the time, place, materials, tools and the agents of magical ceremonies are none other than entry rites for the magical performance, which we also find in sacrifice and which we have described elsewhere. These preliminary rites are of such importance that they constitute separate ceremonies in relation to the ritual they precede. According to the Atharvanic texts, a sacrifice always precedes the rite and supererogatory rites are often performed to prepare the way for each later rite. For Greece, we have long descriptions of special scrolls, spoken and written prayers, diverse talismans which were made to protect the magician against the powers he employed, against inadvertent mistakes and against the machinations of his enemies. While on this subject, we might also include other ceremonies as entry rites, ceremonies which can play a role out of all proportion to the importance of the central rite, designed to achieve the ritual objective. These include ritual dances, continuous music, drumming, fumigation and drug-taking. All these practices aim at inducing special states in the officiants and their clients, not only morally and psychologically, but also physically in some cases. These transformations are realized to perfection in shamanistic trances, voluntary and induced reveries, which also are considered to be part of the ritual. The frequency and importance of such practices show that magical rites take place in a differentiated magical milieu. Preparatory rites performed before the main ceremony mark off and circumscribe this magical milieu from the normal outside world. If the worst comes to the worst a simple action, such as a whisper, a word, a gesture or a look, may suffice to indicate this difference.

As in sacrifice, there are regularly, if not invariably, exit rites— ceremonies designed to limit the effects of a ritual and assure the immunity of the actors. Unused ritual materials are thrown away or destroyed; the people are bathed; participants leave the magical spot without looking behind them. These are not simply individual precautions but are prescribed actions. In Cherokee and Atharvanic ritual, rules of this type are expressly mentioned, and they must also have played a part in the magical rites of the Greco-Romans. Virgil remembers to mention them at the end of the eighth eclogue (v, 102):

> Fer cineres, Amarylli, foras, rivoque fluenti
> Transque caput jace; nec respexeris . . .

In the Μαντεία Κρονική there is a rite of divination and the liturgy has been preserved in the great magical Papyrus of Paris; here again we find a final prayer which is a true exit rite. As a general rule, it seems that magic tends to multiply the elements involved in ritual, to such an extent that it seems to be providing itself with loop-holes, and often successfully. Literary traditions concerning magic, far from reducing the apparently complex nature of these practices, seem to have embroidered on them at will. This is perfectly in accord with our notion of magic. It is natural for a magician to take refuge behind questions of procedure and technicalities, to protect himself in case of failure in magical prowess. Nevertheless, it would be wrong to try and prove that magic simply involves artifice. If this were so the magician would have fallen the victim first and his profession would have become an impossible one. The importance and wide diffusion of these rites point directly at the essential characteristics of magic itself. It is a noteworthy fact that most of the conditions which must be observed are abnormal ones. However commonplace, the magical rite has to be thought of as unique. It is not pure chance that herbs are plucked on the days of St John or St Martin, at Christmas or on Good Friday or at the time of the new moon. These are times which are in themselves extraordinary, and all magical rites generally aim at endowing the ceremonies with an abnormal character. All movements are the opposite of normal ones, particularly those performed at religious ceremonies. Conditions, including those of time, are apparently unrealizable: materials are preferably unclean and the practices obscene. The whole thing is bizarre, involving artifice and unnatural features—very far removed from that simplicity to which recent theorists have wished to reduce magic.

2 *The nature of the rites* We now come to the central rites, those which are directly effective. They usually comprise two types of rite—verbal and non-verbal. Apart from this very broad division, we do not wish to make any further classification of magical ritual. For the benefit of our exposition we shall simply present groups of rites, remembering that between each of these groups there is no well-marked distinction.

Non-verbal rites In the present state of the science of religion, the first group of rites which is given a particularly magical character is that known as sympathetic or symbolic magic. Theoretical contributions to this type of magic have been so extensive and the

repertoire of evidence so considerable that we need not dwell long
on it ourselves. Reading the evidence, one may well believe that the
number of symbolic rites is theoretically endless and also that all
symbolic actions, by their nature, are effective. We, on the contrary,
postulate, without actually having the proof, that in any system of
magic the number of symbolic rites which are prescribed and performed is always limited. We also hold that they are performed, not
because they are logically realizable, but because they are prescribed.
Compared with the infinity of possible symbolic actions, or even
those actually found throughout the world, the number used in a
single magical system is singularly limited. We would be able to
assert that symbolic systems are always limited by codes if we could
find genuine catalogues of sympathetic rites. Naturally enough,
however, these catalogues do not exist, since magicians have only
ever felt the need to classify their rites according to their aims, not
according to their procedures.

We should like to add that, while sympathetic procedures are
employed generally in all magical systems throughout the world,
and while genuine sympathetic ritual does exist, magicians on the
whole have shown no inclination to speculate on the nature of this
sympathy. They are less occupied with the mechanics of the rites
than with the lore which has come down to them and their formal
or exceptional character.

This is why these practices appear to us more like holy actions
and genuine ritual, rather than gestures which are mechanically
effective. Of all the rituals we know—Hindu, American or Greek—
it would be very difficult to pinpoint those which are purely
sympathetic. The variations played on the sympathetic theme are so
great that the whole subject has become obscure.

Of course, magic does not consist entirely of sympathetic rites.
First we have a whole class of rites which can be equated with those
rituals of consecration and deconsecration which we find in religion.
Purificatory systems are so important that the Hindu *shânti*
(expiation) seems to have been a speciality of the Brahmans of the
Atharva Veda. In Greek the word καθαρμός finally came to be
used to mean magical ritual in general. Such purifications are
carried out by fumigations, steam-baths, passing through fire or
water. Many curative rites and ritual to ward off evil are performed
by similar practices.

We next come to sacrificial ritual. We have some in the

Μαντεία Κρονική which we mentioned earlier and also in Hindu magic. In the Atharvaric texts, apart from the obligatory entry rites, the greater part of the ritual involves sacrifice either actually or implicitly. Thus the medicating of arrows is done on a fire of wood used for making arrows; in this kind of ritual a part of everything which is consumed is perforce sacrificial. In the Greek texts hints of sacrifice are fairly frequent. The image of sacrifice has been imposed on magic to such an extent that it has become a kind of guideline, by which the whole procedure is ordered in the mind. In the Greek texts on alchemy, for example, we find over and over again that the transmutation of copper into gold is explained by a sacrificial allegory. The theme of sacrifice, particularly of children, is common enough in our knowledge of the magic of the ancient world and also the Middle Ages, and we have examples of the same kind of thing almost everywhere, although they may be preserved in myths rather than in actual magical practices. We consider all such rites to be sacrifices simply because they are said by the performers to be such. They are not verbally distinguished from religious sacrifice any more than purificatory magic is to be distinguished from purification in religion. Moreover, their effects are the same as those of religious sacrifice, in so far as they release forces and powers and they are a means of communicating with these powers. In the Μαντεία Κρονική the god is even present at the ceremony. The text also explains that, in magical rites, the materials involved are really transformed, assuming a sacred nature. We read in one spell, which seems to have avoided Christian influence:

Σὺ εἶ οἶνος οὐκ εἶ οἶνος, ἀλλ' ἡ κεφαλὴ τῆς 'Αθηνᾶς, σὺ εἶ οἶνος, οὐκ εἶ οἶνος, ἀλλά τὰ σπλάγχνα τοῦ 'Οσείριος, τὰ σπλάγχνα τοῦ 'Ιαώ.

(*Papyrus*, 121, B.M., 710.)

We therefore find that magic and sacrifice may be associated together but this does not apply everywhere. Among the Cherokee Indians and the Australian aborigines sacrifice is completely lacking, and in Malaysia the relationship is tenuous. We have the offering of incense and flowers, which is probably of Buddhist or Hindu origin, and the very rare sacrifice of goats and cocks, which often seems to be of Muslim origin. On the whole, if there is no sacrifice in religion it is also lacking in magic. In any case, a special study of sacrifice in magic is not so relevant to the study of magic as sympathetic ritual and we prefer to reserve this to another work which is to be devoted to a comparison of magical and religious rites. Meanwhile we may merely suggest, as a general thesis, that sacrifice does not form in magic, as it does in religion, a tightly knit class of highly specialized rites. On the one hand, as we saw in the example of the sacrifice of the arrow, by definition, in all cases of expiatory magical sacrifice, sacrifice only dresses up sympathetic rites; it provides, so to speak, the framework of the ritual. On the other hand, it is part of the magical *cuisine*. It is no more than one way, among a thousand others, of performing it. Thus in Greek magic, the confection of the κολλούρια is not distinguished from sacrifice. The papyri call these magical mixtures which are used in fumigations and all kinds of other things by the name of ἐπιθύματα.

We are now confronted with a large category of poorly defined practices which occupy an important place in magic and its dogmas. They cover the use of substances whose virtues are transmitted through contact; in other words they provide the means of utilizing objects sympathetically. Because they are as curious as they are widespread, they affect the whole of magic by their bizarre nature and provide one of the essential features of its popular image. The magician's shrine is a magic cauldron. Magic is the art of preparing and mixing concoctions, fermentations, dishes. Ingredients are chopped up, pounded, kneaded, diluted with liquids, made into scents, drinks, infusions, pastes, cakes, pressed into special shapes, formed into images: they are drunk, eaten, kept as amulets, used in fumigations. This cuisine, pharmacy, chemistry, what you like to call it, not only causes magical materials to be utilizable, but serves to provide them with a ritual character which contributes in no small way to the efficacy of magic. It is a ritual itself, formalized and hidebound by tradition, and the actions involved are rites. These rites should not be lumped along with those entry rites or concomitant rites involved in a magical ceremony. The preparation of the ingredients and the confection of the products is the main—the central—object of the whole ceremony and has its own entry and exit rites. In sacrifice the preparation of the animal corresponds to this aspect of a magical rite. It is a moment in the ritual.

The art of preparing the materials involves other activities. Magicians prepare images from paste, clay, wax, honey, plaster, metal or papier mâché, from papyrus or parchment, from sand or wood. The magician sculpts, models, paints, draws, embroiders, knits, weaves, engraves. He makes jewellery, marquetry and heaven knows what else. These various activities provide him with representations of gods and demons, dolls for black magic; they are all his symbols. He makes gree-grees, scapulars, talismans, amulets, all of which should be seen as continuing rites.

Verbal rites Normally verbal rites in magic are called spells and we see no reason for not continuing this custom. However we do not wish to imply by this that it is the only kind of verbal ritual in magic. This is far from being the case and the system of verbal magic plays such an important role in magic as a whole that in certain systems it is extremely differentiated. Up till now it has never been given its real due. From many modern descriptions one could easily be led to believe that magic involved only non-verbal actions. Verbal ritual is mentioned only in passing terms and is neglected in favour of lengthy enumerations of the other aspects of the rite. On the other hand, there are texts, such as the Lönnrot on Finnish magic, which contain nothing but incantations or spells. Only rarely are we provided with a sufficiently balanced idea of these two vital features of ritual. W. W. Skeat did it for Malaysian magic and J. Mooney for the Cherokee. In magician's manuals we find that rites are normally interdependent. They are so closely associated that in order to provide a correct notion of a magical ceremony we must study the two concurrently. If one or other of these aspects tends to predominate, it is usually the spells. While it is doubtful whether entirely wordless rituals ever existed there is evidence of a large number of rites which were exclusively oral.

In magic we find almost all the same forms of spoken rite which we found in religion: oaths, wishes, prayers, hymns, interjections, simple formulas. However, for the same reason that we made no attempt to classify non-verbal rites, we shall not place these rites in categories. They do not in fact correspond to well-defined classes of fact. Magic is chaotic and there is hardly ever an exact correlation between the form of the ceremony and its professed object. We find the strangest anomalies: hymns of great holiness used for the most evil purposes.

There is one group of spells which corresponds to what we have called sympathetic magical rites. Some even act sympathetically. It is only a matter of naming the actions or things in order to bring about the sympathetic reaction. In a medical spell or in a rite of exorcization, play is made on words like 'withdraw', 'reject', words for the illness itself or the demon responsible for the evil. Puns and onomatopoeic phrases are among the many ways of combating sickness verbally through sympathetic magic. Another method, which gives rise to a special class of spells, is the mere description of a corresponding non-verbal rite: Πάσσ' ἅμα καὶ λέγε ταῦτα. τὰ Δέλφι δος ὀστία πάσσω (Theocritus, 2, 21). Apparently it was often believed that the description of the rite, or even the mention of its name, was enough to conjure it up and produce effect.

Prayers and hymns as well as sacrifice are involved in magic particularly prayers to gods. Here is a Vedic prayer pronounced, during a simple sympathetic rite aimed at curing dropsy (*Kaucika Sutra* 25, 37 *et seq.*):

> This Asura rules over the gods; indeed the will of king Varuna is truth (comes to pass automatically); from this (this illness) I, who excel on all sides by my spell, from the fury of the terrible [god] I remove this man. Let honour [be paid] to you, Oh king Varuna, to your fury; because, terrible one, all deceit is known to you. A thousand other men I will abandon unto you; that through your goodness [?] this man should live one hundred autumns. . . .

Varuna, god of the waters, who punishes evil with dropsy, is evoked as a matter of course during this hymn (Atharva Veda 1, 10), or more exactly during the course of this formula (Brahman, line 4). In prayers to Artemis and the sun, which have been found in Greek magic papyri, the beautiful, lyrical tenor of the invocations is perverted and suffocated by the intrusion of the usual magical hotchpotch. Prayers and hymns, once they are disencumbered from this usual paraphernalia, are very similar to the hymns we are in the habit of calling religious. They are often, in fact, borrowed from religious ritual, especially from prohibited or foreign religions. A. Dieterich has been able to uncover a whole section of Mithraic liturgy in the Great Papyrus of Paris. In the same way sacred texts which are religious in nature may, on occasion, become magical. Holy books, such as the Bible, the Koran, the Vedas, the Tripitakas, have provided spells for a goodly proportion of mankind. We should not be surprised, therefore, if spoken rites of a religious nature are used so extensively in modern magic. This fact is to be correlated with the use of spoken rites in religious practices in the same way as the application of techniques of sacrifice in magic is to be correlated with its use in religion. For any one society there can be only a limited number of conceivable ritual forms.

What the purely non-verbal rites in magic normally do not include is the tracing out of myths. However, there is a third group of verbal rites which comprises mythical spells. Amongst these we have a type of incantation which describes a situation similar to that which the magician is trying to produce. The description usually involves a fairy story or an epic tale, with heroic or divine characters. The actual case is assimilated to one described as if it were a prototype, the reasoning behind it being something like this: if a certain person (a god, saint or hero) was able to do such and such a thing (usually a very difficult task) in such and such a circumstance, perhaps he could perform the same feat in the present case, which is exactly similar. A second type of mythical spell consists of rites which have been called 'original' rites. These describe the genesis and enumerate the names and characteristics of the being, thing or demon concerned in the rite. It is a kind of investigatory process by which the demon involved in the spell is slowly uncovered. The magician institutes magical proceedings, establishes the identity of the powers involved, catches hold of them and brings them under control by the use of his own power.

All these spells may achieve considerable dimensions. However, it is more common for them to shrink in size: the onomatopoeic muttering of a phrase, the naming of the person involved, may indicate the aim of a rite and be performed as a matter of form after the verbal rite has long since become merely an automatic action. Prayers may be reduced to the name of a god or demon, or a well-nigh meaningless ritual word, such as the *trisagion* of the *godesch*, etc. Mythical spells end up by consisting of nothing but a single proper name or a common word. The names themselves become unrecognizable. They may be replaced by letters: *trisagion* becomes a T, the names of planets become vowels. We even get enigmas like the Ἐφέσια γράμματα, or bogus algebraical formulae to which accounts of alchemical procedures are reduced.

All verbal rituals tend to have the same form, because their function tends also to be the same. Their intention is primarily to evoke spiritual forces or to specialize a rite. The magician invokes, conjures up, calls down powers which make rites work; at the very least he feels the need to mention which of the forces he is using.

This occurs when exorcizing rites are carried out in the name of such and such a god; the authority is called in evidence, particularly in mythical charms. Other magicians talk about the objectives of the non-verbal rites, mentioning the name of the person for whom it is being performed. They inscribe or pronounce the name of the victim over the figurine. While collecting certain medicinal herbs they must say for what or for whom they are intended. In this way the spoken rite may render the mechanical rite more complete, more precise, and it may on occasion entirely supplant it. Every ritual action, moreover, has a corresponding phrase, since there is always a minimal representation through which the nature and object of the ritual is expressed, even if this is achieved only through an interior language. It is for this reason that there is no such thing as a wordless ritual; an apparent silence does not mean that inaudible incantations expressing the magician's will are not being made. From this point of view, the mechanical rite is but a translation of the unspoken incantation: a gesture is a sign, and also a language. Words and actions become absolutely equivalent and that is why we find descriptions of the non-verbal rites presented to us as spells. Without any formal physical movement a magician can create, annihilate, direct, hunt, do anything he wishes with the aid of his voice, his breath, or merely through his will.

The fact that all spells are formulas and that virtually all non-verbal rites also have their formulas shows at once to what degree all magic is formalistic. As for the spells themselves, there has never been any doubt that they are rites, since they are traditional, formal and clothed in an effectiveness which is *sui generis*. It has never been suggested that words can physically produce the desired effects. For non-verbal rites this fact is less obvious since there may be a very close parallel, often a logical one, between the rite and the desired effect. Obviously steam-baths and magical anointing have been able to relieve afflicted persons. Nevertheless, the two types of rites have the same characteristics and lend themselves to similar observations. Both take place in an abnormal world.

Spells are composed in special languages, the language of the gods and spirits or the language of magic. Two striking examples of this kind of rite are the Malaysian use of *bhàsahantu* (spirit language) and the Angekok language of the Eskimoes. In Greece, Jamblique informs us that Ἐφέσια γράμματα is the language of the gods. Magicians used Sanskrit in the India of the Prakrits, Egyptian and

Hebrew in the Greek world, Greek in Latin-speaking countries and Latin with us. All over the world people value archaisms and strange and incomprehensible terms. From the very beginnings, practitioners of magic (and perhaps the earliest are to be found in Australia) have mumbled their *abracadabras*.

The peculiar and weird nature of non-verbal ritual is paralleled by the enigmatic mutterings of spoken rites. Far from being the simple expression of individual emotions, magic takes every opportunity to coerce actions and locutions. Everything is fixed and becomes precisely determined. Rules and patterns are imposed. Magical formulas are muttered or sung on one note to special rhythms. Both in the *Catapatha brâhmana* and in Origen we find that intonation is sometimes more important than the actual words. Gestures are regulated with an equally fine precision. The magician does everything in a rhythmical fashion as in dancing: and ritual rules tell him which hand or finger he should use, which foot he should step forward with. When he sits, stands up, lies down, jumps, shouts, walks in any direction, it is because it is all pre-scribed. Even when he is alone he is not freer than the priest at his altar. Apart from this there are some general canons which are common to both spoken and mechanical rites: these involve numbers and directions. Movements and words must be repeated a number of times. Not any number of times, but according to sacred and magical numbers, such as 3, 4, 5, 7, 9, 11, 13, 20, etc. Moreover, words are pronounced or actions are performed facing a certain direction, the most common rule being that the magician should face the direction of the person at whom the rite is aimed. On the whole, magical ritual is extraordinarily formal and tends to become more and more so, to the point of extreme mystical preciosity—the tendency does not lie in the simplicity of everyday actions.

The simplest magical rites have the same form as those which are the object of the greatest number of definitions. Up to now, we have spoken of magic as if it consisted solely of positive actions. There are, however, many negative rites and these are precisely the simple ones which we now mention. We have already noted them in our list of the preparations performed prior to a magical rite—the abstinence required of the magician and the other people involved is a case in point. They also include that huge mass of facts we call superstitions. They consist mainly of avoiding certain actions in order to prevent a magical effect. Here the rites are formal, and formal to a superlative degree, because the imperative character of the rite is almost complete. The kind of obligations associated with these rites show that they are the result of social forces even more than other rites which we have shown to be so because of their traditional, abnormal or formalist characteristics. However, on the important question of sympathetic taboos—negative magic as we prefer to call it—we have so far found so little enlightenment in the work of our predecessors, and also in our own researches, that we are hardly in a position to do more than call attention to the subject as offering an important field for study. For the moment we shall confine our attention to noting that these facts provide yet another proof that ritual—as an element in magic—is predetermined by collective forces.

As for positive rites, we have already pointed out how universally limited they are in each magical system. Their composition—and here we mean the combined effects of spells, negative ritual, sacrifices, recipes—is no less limited. There is a tendency for a limited series of stable complexes to grow up—we call them types of ceremonies—which are quite comparable either to technical patterns or what are known as art styles. There is a choice between available forms in each magical system; but once formulated we find the same clearly marked complexes over and over again, used for all kinds of purposes, no matter the logic of their composition. An example would be the variation on the theme of conjuring up the witch through the objects upon which she has cast a spell. When it is a matter of milk failing to produce butter, the milk in the vat is stabbed with a dagger, a custom which is also carried out to ward off many other kinds of evil. Here we have one type of magical rite and not the only one which furnishes an example on this theme. We also have the medication of two or three dolls, which can be justified only by a similar proliferation. These actions through their persistence and their formalism are comparable to religious ceremonies.

Arts and crafts have styles which might be called tribal or, more precisely, national. In the same way it could also be maintained that each magical system has its own recognizable style which is characterized by the predominance of certain types of ritual: the use of dead men's bones in Australian sorcery, fumigation with tobacco in America, the benedictions and credos of the Muslims and Jews and other magical systems influenced by the religions of these

E

last two. The Malays seem to have been the only people to know the curious ritual theme involving assemblies.

While it is true that different societies exhibit specific styles of magic, within each system—or, from another perspective, within each of the larger ritual groups we have described separately—there are important variations. The choice of the type of magic to be used is partly a matter for specialist magicians who use one rite or a limited number of rites in all the cases for which they are qualified. Each magician is bound by his materials, his tools and his medicine bag, which he inevitably uses every time he works. More often than not a magician is set apart from his colleagues by the type of rites he performs, rather than by the powers he possesses. We might add that the people we have called amateur magicians have an even more limited knowledge of rites and tend to go on repeating the same ones endlessly. This is the reason why certain formulas which are used over and over again, without rhyme or reason, end up by becoming completely unintelligible. Once again we find form taking precedence over content.

Nevertheless, what we have just said on the formation of styles in magical ritual does not mean that they are in fact classifiable. Apart from the question of the existence of a vast amount of floating ritual, the fact remains that the development of special styles is quite a matter of accident and does not correspond to any real diversity of function, in magic there is nothing properly comparable to religious institutions.

3 Representations

Magical practices are not entirely without sense. They correspond to representations which are often very rich and which constitute the third element of magic. As we have seen, all ritual is a kind of language; it therefore translates ideas.

The minimum of display which each magical act involves is display of its effect. But this display, however rudimentary it may conceivably be, is already highly complex. It has several components, several levels. We can indicate at least some of these, so that subsequent analysis will not be purely theoretical; for there are magical systems which are perfectly conscious of their diversity and refer to it with special words and metaphors.

In the first place, we assume that magicians and their followers will not represent the special effects of the rite concerned without taking into account, at least unconsciously, the general effects of magic. Each magical rite seems to have arisen from some kind of syllogistic reasoning with the major term perfectly clearly expressed sometimes even in the spell: *Venenum veneno vincituri natura naturam vincit.* 'We know where you come from. . . . How can you kill like this?' (*Atharva Veda*, vii, 76, 5, *vidma vai te . . . janam . . . Kaltham ha tatra tvám hano . . .*). No matter how different the results of each rite, when they are working, they are thought to have common characteristics. In every case, in fact, we have either the imposing or suppressing of a characteristic or a circumstance: from being bewitched to being delivered, from possession to exorcization. In a simple word there has been a change of state. We are prepared to claim that all magical acts are represented as producing one of two effects: either the objects or beings involved are placed in a state so that certain movements, accidents or phenomena will inevitably occur, or they are brought out of a dangerous state. The actions vary according to the initial state of the individual, the circumstances determining the significance of the change, and the special ends assigned to them. Nevertheless, they share one feature in that their immediate and essential effect is to modify a given state. The magician, therefore, knows full well that his magic is consequently always the same. He is always conscious that magic is the art of changing—the *máyá* as the Hindus call it.

However, apart from this quite formal conception, there are other more concrete elements behind a magical rite. Things come and depart: the soul comes back to the body, fever is driven away. An attempt is made to make sense of an accumulation of images. The bewitched person is ill, lame, imprisoned. Somebody has broken his bones, dried up his marrow, peeled off his skin. The favourite image is of something holding him, and it is tied or untied: 'an evil thread which has been maliciously tied', 'a chaining up which has been etched on the earth', etc. Among the Greeks the spell is a κατάδεσμος, a φιλτροκατάδεσμος. The same idea is expressed in Latin, although more abstractly, in the word *religio*, which has the same meaning. In a spell directed against a type of throat disease, we read, after an enumeration of technical and descriptive terms: *Hanc religionem evoco, educo, excanto de istis membris, medullis*

(Marcellus, 15, 11); *religio* is here treated as a kind of vague being, with a diffuse personality that can be chased and caught. Elsewhere, the effects of the rite are expressed in ethical images: peace, love, seduction, fear, justice, ownership. This kind of representation, whose features are now and then vaguely glimpsed, may also be condensed into distinct notions and given special terms. The Assyrians expressed the idea through the word *mâmit*; in Melanesia, the equivalent of *mâmit* is *mana*, which is seen as a product of the rite; among the Iroquois (Huron) the substance thrown by the magician is called *orenda*; in ancient India it was the *brahman* (neuter) which worked. We call it a charm, enchantment or a spell and the words we use show how unscientific the idea is. The idea is represented as a concrete, material object; a spell or a rune is thrown down, a charm is washed, drowned or burnt.

A third moment in our total representation comes when it is believed that there is a certain relationship between the persons and things involved in the ritual. This relationship may be conceived as a sexual one. An Assyro-Babylonian spell creates a kind of mystical marriage between demons and the images meant to represent them: 'People, evil and wicked ones who have taken off N., son of N., and will not let him go, if you are male let this be your wife, if you are female let this be your husband.' (C. Fossey, *La Magie assyrienne*, Paris, 1902, p. 133.) There are a thousand other ways of conceiving this relationship. It may be represented as something which is shared between the magicians and their victims. The magicians can be reached through their victim who thus has a hold over them. In the same way a spell can be removed by bewitching the magician who, for his part, naturally has control over his own spell. It is also said that it is the magician, or his soul, or his demon which has possessed the victim; in this way he gains control of his victim. Demoniacal possession is the strongest expression, simple spell-binding the weakest, with regard to the relations established between the magician and the subject of his rite. There is a distinct idea that there is a kind of continuity between the agents, the patients, the materials, the spirits and the end-object of a magical rite. Taking everything into consideration, we find the same idea in magic which we found in sacrifice. Magic involves a terrific confusion of images, without which, to our way of thinking, the rite itself would be inconceivable. In the same way that the central person in the sacrifice, the animal victim, god and the sacrifice itself become merged into one, the magician, the magical rite and its effects give rise to a motley of indissociable images. Moreover, this very confusion may be the object of the representation. However separate the different moments in the representation of a magical rite may be, they also form part of a total representation whereby cause and effect become confused. Here we have the basic idea behind magical actions, an idea involving immediate and limitless effects, the idea of direct creation. It is the absolute illusion, the *mâyâ* as the Hindus so aptly named it. Between a wish and its fulfilment there is, in magic, no gap. This is one of its distinctive traits as we see in fairy tales. All those representations which we have been describing are only different forms, different moments, if you like, in this idea of magic. However, there do exist more straightforward representations of magic and these we shall attempt to describe now.

We shall classify these representations as impersonal and personal according to whether the idea of individual beings is involved or not. The first group may be further divided into abstract and concrete classes; the second group, of course, will be only concrete.

1 *Abstract, impersonal representations. The laws of magic*   Impersonal representations of magic involve laws which have been proposed, either implicitly or explicitly, at least in the case of alchemists and doctors. Over the past few years a great deal of importance has been given to these types of representation. It was believed that magic was dominated by them and the quite natural conclusion was reached that magic was a kind of science; when laws are involved we have science. In fact, magic gives every outward appearance of being a gigantic variation on the theme of the principle of causality. But this teaches us nothing, since it would be quite remarkable if it were otherwise, because magic's exclusive aim, apparently, is to produce results. On this subject we can only concede that if its formulas were simplified, it would be impossible not to consider magic as a scientific discipline, a primitive science—and this is exactly what Frazer and Jevons have done. Magic can also function as a science and take the place of sciences not yet developed. The scientific character of magic has been observed throughout the world and has been consciously cultivated by magicians. This tendency towards a scientific orientation is naturally more obvious in the superior forms of magic, those which presuppose a

body of acquired knowledge or refined techniques and which are performed in cultures where the idea of positive science is already present.

From the tangle of changing images it is possible to extract three principal laws. They could in fact all come under the heading of laws of sympathy, if antipathy is also covered by the notion of sympathy. These are the laws of contiguity, similarity and opposition: things in contact are and remain the same—like produces like—opposites work on opposites. E. B. Tylor and others after him have noticed that these laws are none other than the association of ideas (among adults, we would add), with one difference, that here the subjective association of ideas leads to the conclusion that there is an objective association of facts, or in other words that the fortuitous connexion between thoughts is equivalent to the causal connexion between things. If the three principles were to be combined into one, we could state that contiguity, similarity and contrariety equal simultaneity, identity and opposition, in both thought and deed. But we should be left wondering whether these formulas exactly reflect the way in which these so-called laws have been conceived.

Let us first look at the law of contiguity. The simplest expression of the notion of sympathetic contiguity is the identification of a part with the whole. The part stands for the complete object. Teeth, saliva, sweat, nails, hair represent a total person, in such a way that through these parts one can act directly on the individual concerned, either to bewitch or enchant him. Separation in no way disturbs the contiguity; a whole person can even be reconstituted or resuscitated with the aid of one of these parts: *totum ex parte*. It is not necessary to give examples of beliefs which have become so well known by now. The same law may be expressed in another way: the personality of a being is indivisible, residing as a whole in each one of its parts.

This formula applies not only to people but also to things. In magic the essence of an object is found in a piece of it, as well as in the whole. The law is therefore, very general and concerns a property, which is attributed to both the individual's soul and the spirit essence of objects. This is not all: each object contains, in its entirety, the essential principle of the species of which it forms a part. Every flame contains fire, any bone from a dead body contains death, in just the same way as a single hair is thought to contain a man's life force. These observations lead us to believe that we are not only concerned with concepts involving an individual's soul; thus, the law cannot be explained by properties which are implicitly attributed to souls. Neither is it a complementary aspect of a life theory concerning life tokens. A belief in life tokens, on the contrary, is only a special case of *totum ex parte*.

This law of contiguity, moreover, comprises other features. Everything which comes into close contact with the person—clothes, footprints, the imprint of the body on grass or in bed, the bed, the chair, everyday objects of use, toys and other things, all are likened to different parts of the body. There is no need for contact to be permanent or frequent, or actually made—as in the case of clothes or objects of everyday use. A road, objects touched by mere accident, bath water, a fruit that has been bitten into, etc.—all can be used magically. Magic performed over the residues of meals —which is practised throughout the world—follows from the idea that there is a continuity and complete identity between the remains, the food consumed and the one who has eaten—the latter being substantially identical to the food partaken by him. A similar relationship of identity exists between a man and his family. It is through his relatives that he can be harmed most effectively and it is always deemed a useful practice to name them in spells or to write their names on magical objects designed to bring him harm. The same relationship exists between a man and his domestic animals, his house, roof, fields, etc. There is also continuity between a wound and the weapon that caused it: a sympathetic relationship is involved in the curing of the wound through the intermediacy of the weapon. The same tie links a murderer and his victim. The notion of sympathetic continuity leads to a belief that the corpse bleeds when the assassin approaches it. It returns immediately to the state it was in at the time of the crime. The explanation of this phenomenon is a valid one, since we have several clear examples of this kind of continuity. It even spreads further than the guilty one. It was believed, for example, that if a man maltreated a robin-redbreast his cows would give forth red milk (Simmenthal, Switzerland).

As a result, we find that both individuals and objects are theoretically linked to a seemingly limitless number of sympathetic associations. The chain is so perfectly linked and the continuity such that, in order to produce a desired effect, it is really unimportant whether magical rites are performed on any one rather than another of the connexions. Sidney Hartland says that a girl, deserted by her lover, may make him suffer sympathetically by winding some of her hair round the feet of a frog or, alternatively, twining it into a cigar (Lucques). In Melanesia (the New Hebrides and the Solomon Islands, apparently) the friends of a man who has wounded another are placed in a position, as a result of the blow itself, of poisoning the victim's wound by magic.

The idea of magical continuity, realized through the relationship between parts and the whole or through accidental contact, involves the idea of contagion. Personal characteristics, illness, life, luck, every type of magical influx are all conceived as being transmitted along a sympathetic chain. Although contagion is already one of the best known of all magical and religious notions, we shall spend a little time on the idea. In cases of imaginary contagion, a fusion of images is produced in exactly the same way as we found in sacrifice. The result is relative identification of the things and beings in contact. In a manner of speaking, it is the image of the thing to be displaced that runs along the sympathetic chain. This fact is often a feature of the rite itself. In India the victim must touch the magician at a certain moment in the main rite; in Australia the person being medicated has a thread or chain attached to him and the illness is chased along it. However, magical contagion is not only an ideal which is limited to the invisible world. It may be concrete, material and in every way similar to physical contagion. In order to diagnose maladies, Marcellus of Bordeaux advised patients to be sent to bed for a period of about three days with a puppy which had not yet been taken away from its mother. The patient had to give the dog milk from his own mouth and at frequent intervals (*ut aeger ei lac de ore suo frequenter infundat*), after which all that remained to be done was to open the dog's belly. Marcellus adds that the death of the dog cured the man. An exactly similar rite is practised among the Baganda of central Africa. In both cases the fusion of images is perfect. More than an illusion is involved—there is also hallucination. You can really see the illness leaving the person and being transmitted elsewhere. Here we have a transfer—rather than an association—of ideas.

Such a transference of ideas is further complicated by the transference of sentiments. From beginning to end in a magical rite we find the same sentiment, which gives sense and style to the ceremony, and which, in all truth, directs and orders the associations of ideas. This is the factor which explains how the law of continuity functions in magical rites.

In most applications of the law of sympathy through contiguity, it is not merely a matter of spreading a quality or state from one object or person to another. If the law, as we have formulated it, were absolute, or if—in those magical rites where it functions—it were the sole factor involved (and then only in its intellectual form) and if we are in fact only concerned with the association of ideas, then we would be able to state at once that all the elements of a magical chain—constituted by an infinity of possible, necessary or accidental contacts—would be equally affected by the quality they were engaged in transmitting and, consequently, that all the qualities of any element in the chain, whatever they were, would be transmitted *in toto* to each other part. This, however, is not the case; if it were, magic would be impossible. The effects of sympathetic magic are always limited to the effects desired. On the one hand, the current of sympathy is interrupted at precise points. On the other, only a jingle transmissible quality or, at the most, only a few, are transmitted. Thus, when the magician absorbs his client's illness, he himself does not become ill. Similarly, he communicates only the everlasting nature of the powder taken from a mummy which is used to prolong life, the value of gold or diamonds, the insensitivity of a dead man's tooth. Contagion is limited to those properties which the magician detaches and abstracts from the whole.

It is even held that by their very nature the properties in question are localized in one spot. A man's good fortune, for example, is to be found in the straw of his thatched hut. From the idea of localization derives that of separability. The ancient Greeks and Romans thought that they could cure eye diseases by transmitting a lizard's sight to an afflicted individual. The lizard has his eyes put out and is then brought into contact with pebbles which are used as amulets. In this way its sight, cut off at the roots, could be made to go, in its entirety, wherever the magician wished. Separation and abstraction are expressed, in this example, by these rites; but this care is not always necessary.

Those limitations which are placed on the theoretical effects of the law are the real condition of its application. The same requirements which make the rite work and lead to the association of ideas also determine their selection and limitation. Thus in all cases where the abstract notion of magical contiguity functions, the association of ideas is accompanied by transfer of sentiments, by phenomena of abstraction and exclusive attention, and by direction of intent: phenomena which take place in the consciousness, but which are objectivized in the same way as the association of ideas themselves.

The second law, the law of similarity, has a less direct expression than the first as far as ideas of sympathy are concerned. We think Frazer was right when he, along with Sidney Hartland, reserved the term sympathy proper for phenomena including contagion, and called this other category, which we shall now deal with, 'mimetic sympathy'. This law of similarity has two principal formulas which it is important to distinguish: like produces like, *similia similibus evocantur*; and like acts upon like, and, in particular, cures like, *similia similibus curantur*.

As far as the first of these formulae is concerned, it amounts to saying that similarity equals contiguity. The image is to the object as the part is to the whole. In other words, a simple object, outside all direct contact and all communication, is able to represent the whole. This is the formula which is apparently used in black magic. However, it is not simply the idea of an image which is at work here. The similitude which comes into play is, in fact, quite conventional; there is nothing resembling a portrait. The only thing the image and the victim have in common is the convention which associates the two. The image, the doll or the drawing is a very schematic representation, a poorly executed ideogram. Any resemblance is purely theoretical or abstract. The law of similarity, therefore, when it is working, like the preceding law presupposes the existence of phenomena of abstraction and attention. Assimilation does not derive from any illusion. Moreover, these images are dispensable. The mere mention of a name—even thinking it, the slightest rudiment of mental assimilation—is sufficient for an arbitrarily chosen substance—bird, animal, branch, cord, bow, needle, ring—to represent the victim. The image is, therefore, defined only through its function which is simply to produce the person. The basic thing is that the function of representation should be fulfilled. From this it follows that the object to which this function is attributed may be changed for another during the course of a ceremony or that the function itself may be divided between several objects. If one wishes to blind an enemy by passing one of his hairs through the eye of a needle, which has sewn up three shrouds, and then sticking holes in the eye of a toad with the same needle, the hair and the toad are both used in turn as *volt*. As Victor Henry has remarked on the subject of a Brahmanical magical rite, a single lizard may, at various points in the rite, represent the curse, the person uttering the curse and the evil contained in the curse.

In the same way as the law of contiguity, the law of similarity can be applied not only to persons and their souls but also to objects and modes of objects, in their possible and real aspects and their moral and material ones. The idea of the image—as it becomes more extensive—assumes the nature of a symbol. Rain, thunder, sun, fever and unborn children may be symbolically represented by poppy flowers, an army by a doll, a village union by a pot of water, love by a knot, etc., and they are created through their representations. The fusion of images is complete for these cases as well as the earlier ones, since it is not an imaginary wind, but the real wind which is found enclosed in a bottle or goatskin, tied in knots or encircled by rings.

On top of this application, the law results in a whole series of interpretations which are quite remarkable. In the determination of symbols, in their utilization, we have the same phenomena of exclusive attention and abstraction without which we should be unable to conceive of the application of the laws of similarity—as exemplified in the images used in black magic—nor the functioning of the law of continuity. Of the objects chosen as symbols the magicians are concerned with but a single quality, for example in clay—its coolness, weight, its leaden colour, its hardness or softness. The needs and propensities of the rites not only determine the choice of symbols and the use to which they are put, but also limit the consequences of assimilation, which theoretically, like the series of contiguous associations, ought to be limitless. Moreover, all the qualities of the symbol are never transmitted or symbolized. The magician believes himself in control, to be able to channel at will the effects of his actions. He is able, for example, to restrict the effects of funerary symbols to sleep or blindness. The magician who brings rain is content with a shower, since he fears a deluge. The man who is assimilated to a frog which has had its eyes gouged out does not magically turn into a frog.

This apparently arbitrary business of abstraction and interpretation does not result in an infinite multiplication of possible symbolic structures. On the contrary, we have noticed that the existing scope for lively imaginations in any one magical system seems curiously limited. For one object we have to be content with a single symbol, or at most but a few. More surprisingly, there are only a few objects which can be expressed symbolically. The magical imagination has been uninventive to such an extent that the small number of symbols which have been thought up have been put to manifold uses: magical knots are required to represent love, rain, wind, curing, war, language and a thousand other things. The poverty of the symbolic system is not the creation of single individuals whose dreams, psychologically, would be very free. The individual finds himself confronted by rites and traditional ideas which he is never tempted to refurbish because he has faith in tradition; without tradition there can be no beliefs nor rites. For this reason it is natural that traditional symbols should be meagre.

The second formula of the law of similarity—that like acts on like, *similia similibus curantur*—differs from the first in that, even in its expression, the actors take into account those phenomena of abstraction and attention which always condition, as we pointed out, the application of the other rites. While the first type deals only with general evocations, these rites involve an effect being produced in a well-defined direction. The course of the action is then determined by the rite. Take, for example, the legend of the curing of Iphiclos. One day his father, Phylax, brandished a blood-stained knife at him while they were castrating goats. He was made sterile through the sympathetic effect of this action and failed to have children. When the diviner Melampos was consulted he made Iphiclos drink wine mixed with some rust from the knife which had been recovered from the tree where Phylax had hidden it. This was repeated over ten days. The knife was capable of exacerbating Iphiclos's condition, and at the same time Iphiclos's qualities could pass into the knife through sympathy. Melampos permitted only the latter to take effect, and limited it to the illness in question. In this way the king's sterility was absorbed by the sterilizing power of the instrument. The same thing occurred in India when Brahmans cured dropsy through ablutions. Here the patient was not made to take an overdose of liquid, but the water with which he came into contact absorbed the liquids which were making him suffer.

While these facts can be grouped under the law of similarity, deriving as they do from the abstract notion of mimetic sympathy, of *attractio similium*, their special features cause them to be placed in a class apart. This is more than a corollary of the law; it is a kind of concurrent notion which may equal it in importance owing to the number of rites which it dominates in each ceremony.

Before leaving the exposition of the second form of our law of similarity, we find ourselves face to face with the law of opposition. When like is found to cure like, what we have in fact is the opposite. The sterilizing knife produces fertility, water produces the absence of dropsy, etc. A complete formula for these rites would be: like drives out like in order to produce the opposite. Conversely, as far as the first series of facts involving mimetic sympathy is concerned, when like evokes like it drives away the opposite: when I cause rain to fall by pouring water on the ground I am causing the disappearance of drought. In this way the abstract notion of similarity is inseparable from the abstract notion of contrariety. The two forms of similarity could thus be brought together in one formula, 'opposite drives away opposite', or in other words could be included in the law of opposition.

But this law of opposition has always existed separately in the minds of the magicians. Sympathy may be equated with antipathy, but the two are clearly distinguished from each other. A proof of this is that in antiquity there were books called Περὶ συμπαθείων καὶ ἀντιπαθείων. Whole systems of ritual—involving pharmaceutical magic and counter-spells—can be classed under the idea of antipathy. Magic has always speculated on polarity and opposition: good and bad fortune, cold and hot, water and fire, freedom and coercion. A large number of things have been grouped together in opposites and this opposition has been taken advantage of. We therefore consider the idea of contrast as a distinct idea in magic.

In fact, just as similarity cannot exist without opposition, opposition does not exist without similarity. In an Atharvanic ritual, rain is made to stop by invoking its opposite, the sun, with the aid of a wood known as *arka*, which means light, lightning or sun. In this rite of opposition we can already see the mechanisms of sympathy, properly so called. A further proof that they are not incompatible is that the magician uses the same piece of wood directly to stop storms, thunder and lightning. In both cases the material used in the rite is the same; only their treatment varies slightly. In the one case fire is exposed, in the other glowing coals are buried. This simple ritual modification expresses the will which directs the rite. We can state, therefore, that opposite drives out its opposite by evoking its equivalent.

Thus the separate formulas covered by the law of similarity can all be exactly fitted into the formula of opposition. From the point of view of the ritual schema used in our study of sacrifice, it can be said that symbolic structures are present in three schematic forms, each corresponding to one of three formulas: like produces like; like acts on like; opposite acts on opposite. They differ only in the ordering of their elements. In the first case, we think primarily of the absence of a state; in the second, we are dealing first with the presence of a state; in the third, we are dealing with the presence of a state opposite to that which is desired. In the first, we think in terms of the absence of rain, which has to be produced through a symbol; in the second, we think of falling rain which is made to stop through a symbol; in the third, rain is conjured up and then brought to a stop by evoking its opposite through a symbol. In this way abstract notions of similarity and opposition may both be encompassed by the more general idea of traditional symbolism.

In the same way the laws of similarity and contiguity tend to merge into each other. Frazer has stated the case well, and he could easily have produced proof of it. Rites of similarity normally involve contact: contact between the witch and her clothing, the magician and his wand, a weapon and a wound. The sympathetic effects of a substance are only transmitted by absorption, infusion, touch, etc. Conversely, these contracts are usually only vehicles for qualities of symbolic origin. In black magic, practised with the aid of a person's hair, the hair is a link between the desired destruction and the victim to be destroyed. In an infinity of similar cases we do not find any clear pattern of ideas and rites, but an interweaving of elements. The actions become so complicated that it is only with great difficulty that they can be neatly ordered into one or other of our two categories. In fact, whole series of black magic ritual contain contiguities, similarities and neutralizing oppositions alongside pure similarities, without the magicians bothering about them or really having in mind anything except the final objective of their rite.

Let us now consider the two laws, ignoring their complexities for a moment. First of all, we find that sympathetic (or mimetic) actions performed at a distance are not always thought to be working on their own. There is the idea of effluvia which leave the body, magical images which travel about, lines linking the magician and his field of action, ropes, chains. Even the magician's soul leaves his body to perform the act he has just produced. The *Malleus maleficarum* mentions a witch who dips her broom in a pond to bring on rain and then flies away into the air to search for it. Several Ojibway pictograms depict the priest-magician, after the ritual, holding his arms up to heaven, piercing the vault of the sky and drawing clouds towards him. It is this kind of thing which makes us imagine that similarity is the same as contiguity. On the other hand, contiguity may also be the same as similarity, and with reason: the law holds only when the individuals involved, the substances in contact, in fact the whole ritual ensemble, contain the same circulating essence, which renders them identical. That is why all our abstract, impersonal representations of similarity, contiguity and opposition—even if they may once have been separately conceived—have become naturally confused and confusing. They are obviously three aspects of one idea; and it is this idea we must now set to work and clarify.

Several magicians who concerned themselves with the meaning of their ritual have shown themselves perfectly aware of this confusion. The alchemists had a general principle, which appears to have summed up perfectly their theoretical reflections. They always prefixed it to their schemes: 'Each one is the whole and the whole is in each one'. Here, chosen at random, is a passage which nicely expresses this principle: 'Each one is the whole and it is through it that the whole is formed. One is the whole and if each one did not contain the whole, the whole could not be formed'. Ἐν γὰρ τὸ πᾶν, καὶ δι' αὐτοῦ τὸ πᾶν γέγονε. Ἐν τὸ πᾶν καὶ εἰ μὴ κατέχῃ τὸ πᾶν, οὐ γέγονε τὸ πᾶν. This whole, which is contained in everything, is the world. And we are sometimes told that the world is conceived as a unique animal, whose parts, however disparate they may seem, are inextricably associated. Everything has something in common with everything else and everything is connected with everything else. This kind of magical pantheism provides a synthesis for our different laws. The alchemists, however, never insisted on this formula, except in so far as it provided their studies with a metaphysical or philosophical commentary, of which we have only the remnants today. However, they did insist on one formula which was juxtaposed to the other: *Natura naturam vincit*, etc. It is 'nature', by definition, which is found both in the object and in its parts. Here we have the basis of the law of contiguity, and it is this which is found in all members of a single species and forms the basis of the law of similarity. It is the same thing which enables an object to act on an opposite object of the same kind, and is, therefore, the basis of our law of opposition.

The alchemists did not confine themselves to the field of abstract considerations and it is this fact which proves to us that these ideas really worked in magic. They understood by φύσις, by *nature*, the idea of a hidden essence and their magical water which produced gold. The idea behind these formulas—one which the alchemists never tried to conceal—involves a substance which acts on other substances by virtue of its properties, whatever their mode of action. This action is a sympathetic one or may be produced between sympathetic substances. It can be expressed in the following way: like acts on like; and we should add, along with our alchemists, that like attracts like, or that like dominates like (ἕλκει or κρατεῖ). They say that this is because you cannot act on the whole with the whole. Since nature (φύσις) is disguised in forms (εἴδη), there has to be a convenient relationship between the εἴδη, that is, the forms of the objects which act upon one another. Thus, when they say 'nature triumphs over nature' they mean that there are objects which have a relationship of such close dependence that they are fatally attracted to each other. It is from this point of view that the nature of the destructive element is to be envisaged. In fact, it is an element which dissociates things, which uses its influence to destroy unstable components, and as a result brings about new phenomena and new forms, attracting to itself those identical and stable elements which they contain.

Have we here a general notion of magic, rather than merely a particular notion associated with one branch of Greek magic? Most probably the alchemists did not invent it. It is found in philosophy and we see it applied in medicine. It also seems to have functioned in Hindu medicine. Whatever the case, it matters little whether the idea was ever consciously expressed elsewhere. It is clear that these abstract representations of similarity, contiguity and opposition are inseparable from ideas of things, natures or properties which are transmissible from one being or object to another. This is all we wish to deduce from the facts. It is also true that these properties and forms resemble different rungs of a ladder, which must be scaled before one can act on *nature*, and that the inventions of the magician are not made freely and that his methods of action are essentially limited.

2 *Concrete impersonal representations* Magical thinking cannot, therefore, thrive on abstraction. We have clearly seen that when the alchemists spoke of nature in general, they were referring to a very special kind of nature. For them it was not a pure idea, covering all the laws of sympathy, but a very distinct representation of effective properties. This brings up the topic of those concrete personal representations which are known as *properties* or qualities. Magical rites can be explained much less clearly through the application of abstract laws than through the transfer of properties whose actions and reactions are known beforehand. Rites of contiguity, by definition, involve the simple transmission of properties. A child who does not speak receives the talkativeness of a parrot; a person with toothache is given the hardness of rodents' teeth. Rites of opposition are not more than struggles between properties of a similar kind, appertaining to different species. Fire is the correct opposite of water and for this reason it can drive away rain. Finally, rites of similarity are such only because they can be reduced, in a manner of speaking, to the sole and absorbing contemplation of a single property: a magician's fire reproduces the sun, because the sun *is* fire.

But this idea of properties is both a very clear one and a very obscure one at the same time—a fact which applies to all magical and religious ideas. In magic and religion the individual does not reason, or if he does his reasoning is unconscious. Just as he has no need to reflect on the structure of his rite in order to practise it, or to understand the nature of his prayers and sacrifice, so he has no need to justify his ritual logically, nor does he worry about the whys and wherefores of the properties he employs, caring very little to justify in a rational manner the choice and use of his materials. We are sometimes able to retrace the secret pathway of his ideas, but he himself is usually incapable of it. In his mind he has only the vaguest idea of a possible action, for which tradition furnishes him with a ready-made means, yet he has an extraordinarily precise idea of the end he wishes to achieve. When he recommends that a woman in child-labour should not let flies buzz around her for fear she should have a daughter, it is believed that flies are endowed with sexual properties whose effects must be warded off. When the cream jug is thrown out of the room in order to bring good weather, the jug is endowed with properties of a certain kind. However, there is no attempt to trace back the chain of associated

F

ideas by which the originators of these rites arrived at their notions.

These kinds of representations are perhaps the most important concrete impersonal representations in magic. The widespread use of amulets attests their extension. A good deal of magical ritual is concerned with manufacturing amulets which, once they have been ritually medicated, can be used without rite. Moreover, a certain type of amulet is made of substances and elements whose appropriation may not have necessitated any ritual. This is true of precious stones, diamonds, pearls, etc., to which magical properties are attributed. However, whether an amulet derives its virtues from ritual or from intrinsic qualities of the material itself, it is fairly certain that when it is used the owner clearly considers only its permanent attribute.

Another fact which shows the importance of the notion of properties in magic is that one of the major preoccupations of magic has been to determine the use and the specific, generic or universal powers of beings, things, even ideas. The magician is a person who, through his gifts, his experience or through revelation, understands nature and natures; his practice depends on this knowledge. It is here that magic most approximates science. From this point of view, magic can be very knowledgeable even if it is not truly scientific. A good deal of the knowledge we have mentioned here has been acquired and verified through experiment. Sorcerers were the first poisoners, the first surgeons—we are aware that primitive surgery can be highly developed. Magicans made real discoveries in the field of metallurgy. However, unlike those theorists who have compared magic to science, because of the abstract representations of sympathy sometimes found in the former, it is because of the magician's speculations and observations on the concrete properties of things that we are willing to accord him the title of scientist. The laws of magic discussed above are really a kind of magical philosophy. They were a series of empty, hollow forms bringing in laws of causality which were always poorly formulated. Now, thanks to the notion of property, we have come across rudiments of scientific laws, involving necessary and positive relationships thought to exist between certain objects. Owing to the fact that magicians came to concern themselves with contagion, harmonies, oppositions, they stumbled across the idea of causality, which is no longer mystical even when it involves properties which are in no way experimental. From this line of thinking they ended up deriving, in authentic fashion, special properties from words and symbols.

We affirm that each magical system has necessarily set up categories of plants, minerals, animals, parts of the body, dividing them into groups which do or do not have special or experimental properties. On the other hand, each system has set about codifying the properties of abstract things—geometrical figures, numbers, moral qualities, death, life, luck, etc. And the two sets of categories have been made concordant.

Here we come up against an objection: we are told that the laws of sympathy determine the nature of these properties. The properties of such and such a plant, for example, derive from the fact that the object or being on which it is supposed to act has the same—or different—colour. In this case, we must reply that far from there being any association of ideas between the two objects due to their colour, we are dealing, on the contrary, with a formal convention, almost a law, whereby, out of a whole series of possible characteristics, colour is chosen to establish a relationship between two things. Moreover, only one, or very few, of the objects having that colour are chosen to share this relationship. This is how it works among the Cherokee Indians when they choose their 'yellow root' to cure jaundice. This kind of reasoning, applied here to colour, can also be used with regard to form, contrariety and all other possible properties.

Furthermore, while it is clear that objects are vested with particular powers, by virtue of their names (*reseda morbos reseda*), we claim that things act more as incantations than as objects with properties, since they are really kinds of materialized words. In these cases, the conventions we mentioned above come into greater evidence, since we are dealing with that most perfect of all conventions—a word, whose meaning, sound and everything about it, by definition, are all produced through tribal or national consensus. With a little difficulty we might also include in this argument the notion of magical keys, whereby the properties of things are defined through their relations with certain gods or certain things, which in fact represent their power (for example, the hair of Venus, Jupiter's finger, Ammon's beard, a virgin's urine, Shiva's liquid, an initiate's brain, the substance of Pedu). Here the convention which establishes the sympathetic relationship is a double one. First of all we have the convention determining the choice of name for the first sign (urine = Shiva's liquid) and then there is the other which determines the relationship between the named object, the second sign and the effect (Shiva's liquid = cure for fever since Shiva is the god of fever).

The sympathetic relationship is perhaps more apparent in the case of those parallel series of plants, perfumes and minerals which are said to correspond to planets. However, without commenting on the conventional nature of the attribution of the substances to each planet, we should at least take into consideration the convention which determines the virtues of the planets, virtues which are on the whole moral ones (Mars = war, etc). In summary, far from the idea of sympathy being the presiding principle in the formation of ideas concerning properties, it is the notion of property and the social conventions behind the objects which allow the collective spirit to link together the sympathetic bonds concerned.

In overcoming our self-imposed objection in this way, we do not wish to imply that the properties of an object are not a part of a system of sympathetic relationships. Quite the contrary: we hold that the facts we have just mentioned are of the utmost importance. They have been called 'signatures', that is, symbolic correspond-ences. They provide, in our opinion, examples of a classification similar in many ways to those studied in *Année Sociologique* [1948–9?]. Things which are grouped together under this or that astral sign belong to the same class, or rather to the same family, as the astral body, its region, its mansions, etc. Those which have the same colour, the same shape and so on are believed to be related because of their colour, their shape, their sex. The grouping of things by opposites is also a method of classification. It is really a way of thinking which is basic to all magical systems, that is, the division of everything into at least two groups: good and evil, alive and dead. In this way, the system of sympathetic and antipathetic magic can be reduced to one of classifying collective representations. Things affect each other only because they belong to the same class or are opposed in the same genus. It is because they are members of one and the same family that things, movements, beings, numbers, events, qualities gain a reputation for being similar. It is also because they are members of the same class that one can act on another, it being held that a similar nature is common to a whole class, in the same way as the same blood is held to diffuse throughout an entire clan. As a result, they are involved in relations of similarity and continuity. Furthermore, from class to class we find oppositions. Magic becomes possible only because we are dealing with classified species. Species and classifications are themselves collective phenomena. And it is this which reveals both their arbitrary character and the reason why they are limited to such a small number of selected objects. In fact, when we are dealing with representations of magical properties we find ourselves in the presence of phenomena which are comparable to those of language. Just as no object has an infinite number of names, so, with regard to things, the number of signs is restricted. And just as words have only a distant relationship, or none at all, with the things they describe, between a magical sign and the object signified we have very close but very unreal relations—of number, sex or image, qualities which in general are quite imaginary, but imagined by society as a whole.

In magic there are other representations—both impersonal and concrete—besides those of properties. They include representations of the power of the ritual, and its methods of action. We mentioned this earlier in our discussion of the general effects of magic, pointing out the concrete forms of such notions as *mâmit*, *mana*, effluvia, chains, lines, jets of water, etc. We also find representations of the magician's power and his methods of action, also mentioned earlier when discussing the subject of the magician himself: the power in his look, his strength, his presence, his invisibility, his insubmersibility, his power of transportation, his ability to act directly from a distance, etc.

These concrete representations, along with other abstract representations, provide us in themselves with a conception of the magical rite. There are, in fact, numerous rites which consist of no more definite representations than these. The fact that they are sufficient in themselves perhaps provides justification for persons who see magic as the direct working of ritual and who relegate to a subsidiary role those demonological representations which to us, at least, are necessarily found in all magical systems.

3 *Personal representations. Demonology* There is no real discontinuity between those ideas involving spirits and the concrete and abstract ideas we have just been discussing. Between the idea of the spirituality of magical action and the idea of the spirit there is only a small gap to breach. The idea of a personal agent, from this point of view, could be considered as the product of the effort made by the magical efficacity of rites and their qualities, in order

for their expression to be represented concretely. In fact, it has happened that demonology has been considered a means of expressing magical phenomena: the miasmas are devils, αἰ ἀγαθαὶ ἀπόρροιαι τῶν ἀστέρων εἰσὶν δαίμονες καὶ τύχαι καὶ μοῖραι. The idea of the demon, from this point of view, is not inconsistent with other notions. It is in a way a supplementary idea useful in explaining the play of laws and properties. Here we have a simple substitution of the person as a causal factor for the idea of magical causality.

All magical representations may have personal representations. The magician's double and his animal auxiliary are personal expressions of his power and the way his actions work. Some Ojibway pictograms show it as a *manitou* of the Jossakîd. In the same way the miraculous sparrow-hawk which carries out Nectanebo's orders represents his magical powers. In both these cases the attendant demon or animal is the personal and effective agent of the magician. Through it he acts from afar. In the same way the power of the rite may be personalized. In Assyria, the *mâmit* is like a demon. In Greece the ἴυγξ that is, the magical wheel, has conjured up demons, and so do certain magical formulas, such as the *Ephesia grammata*. The idea of properties works the same way. Plants with special virtues are linked to demons who cure as well as bring diseases. We find demons of vegetation of this kind in Melanesia and among the Cherokee, as well as in Europe (the Balkans, Finland, etc.). The bathing devils on Greek vases derive from the practice of using objects from baths in spells. We see from this example that personification can be associated with a minor aspect of the rite. It may equally well be applied to the most general aspects of magical power. In India, *Shakti*, power, is deified. Obtaining such powers, *siddhi*, is also deified. *Siddhi* is invoked, in the same way as the *Siddha*, those who have obtained it.

Personification is not limited to these examples. Even the subject of the rite may be personified by its ordinary name. This applies first of all to illnesses: fever, fatigue, death, destruction, anything in fact which is exorcized. An interesting story could be told of that doubtful divinity of Atharvanic ritual who is known as the goddess Diarrhoea. Naturally, we find the growth of this phenomenon in the system of incantations, particular evocations, rather than in purely non-verbal rites, although they may exist here and remain unobserved. In incantations, the illness which the magician is trying to drive away is addressed and in this way treated as a person. For this reason almost all Malaysian formulas are conceived of as invocations addressed to princes and princesses who are no less than the objects and phenomena involved in the rite. Elsewhere, in the *Atharvaveda* for example, everything magically medicated becomes really personified: arrows, drums, urine. Here we are concerned with something more than a language form. These people are more than simple vocatives. They existed both before and after the incantations were made. They include the Greek φόβοι, the genies of illness in Balkan folklore, *Laksmî* (fortune) and *Nirrti* (destruction) in India. The latter even have their own mythology like other illnesses personified in the majority of magical systems.

The introduction of the idea of spirits does not necessarily modify the magical rite. In the main, spirits in magic are not a free force. They must simply obey the rite, which indicates how they should go about their work. It is, therefore, a possibility that nothing betrays their presence and that they need not even be mentioned in spells. All the same, it often happens that the spiritual auxiliary does play its part, and sometimes a big part, in magical ceremonies. In some, the image of the auxiliary animal or genie is conjured up. We find in ritual and prayers hints of offerings and sacrifices which have no other object than to evoke and satisfy the demands of personal spirits. If truth be told, these rites are frequently supererogatory in relation to the central rite, the schema of which always remains symbolic or sympathetic in its principal lines. Yet they are sometimes so important that they entirely swamp the ceremony. Thus, an exorcism rite may be encapsulated in a sacrifice or a prayer addressed to a demon who is to be driven out, or to a god who drives him away.

In dealing with these kinds of rites, it would be true to say that the notion of the spirits is the pivot on which they turn. It is obvious, for example, that the idea of a demon will take precedence over all other thoughts in the mind of the officiant, when, for example, he addresses a god in Greco-Egyptian magic in order to beg him to send a demon to work for him. In cases like this, the idea of the rite, along with everything involving automatic inevitability, fades into the background. The spirit is an independent servant and assumes, in magical practices, the role of chance. The magician ends up admitting that his science is not an infallible one and that his will is not necessarily accomplished. He is dealing with a power. In the same way the spirit is both a subject and free form, merged with the ritual and separate from the ritual. Here we seem to be in the presence of one of those antinomian confusions which abound in the history of both magic and religion. The understanding of these apparent contradictions belongs to the theory of the relationship of magic and religion. However, we can state here that the most common magical facts include those where the ritual seems to constrain. But we do not wish to deny the existence of other facts, which will be explained elsewhere.

What are magical spirits? We shall attempt a very summary explanation, a very rapid enumeration, in order to show how magic has recruited its bands of spirits. We shall at once find that these spirits have other than magical qualities and that we also come across them in religion.

Our first category of magical spirits embraces the souls of the dead. Magical systems even exist which—either from the beginning or through a process of reduction—have only this kind of spirit. In western Melanesia, people have recourse to spirits known as *tindalos* —all of whom are spirits of the dead—in both their magic and their religion. Any dead person may become a *tindalo*, if he proves his power through the performance of a miracle, a maleficent action, etc. However, in principle, only people who possessed religious or magical powers when alive may become *tindalos*. The dead, in this case, provide the spirits. They do so in Australia and in America as well, among the Cherokee and Ojibway. In ancient and modern India the dead, deified ancestors are invoked during magical ceremonies. In spells, however, the spirits are invoked of dead persons for whom funeral rites have not yet been appropriately performed (*preta*), of those who have not been buried, of those who died a violent death, of women who died in childbirth, of the spirits of stillborn children (*bhûta*, *churels*, etc.). In ancient Greece, the δαίμονες, that is, magical spirits, are given names which indicate that they are souls of the dead. We even have the occasional mention of νεκυδαίμονες or δαίμονες μητρῷοι καὶ πατρῷοι, although they are most frequently those of demons who died a violent death (βιαιοθάνατοι) or who were not buried (ἄποροι ταφῆς), etc. In Greek areas another type of dead person provides magical auxiliaries: these are the heroes, that is, the dead who form the object of a public cult. It is not clear, however, whether all the magical heroes were official ones. On this point the Melanesian *tindalo* may be reasonably compared with the Greek hero, since although he may be a person who was not deified after death, he is necessarily conceived in this way. In Christianity the dead all have properties which may be useful, qualities deriving from their death. However, magic makes use only of the souls of non-baptized children, those who died violent deaths and dead criminals. Even such a short exposition shows that the dead are magical spirits either by virtue of a general belief in their divine powers, or because of their special qualities which, in the phantom world, give them a special role in relation to religious beings.

A second category of magical beings embraces demons. The word 'demon', of course, is not used here as a synonym for devil, but for words such as genie and *djinn*. Demons are spirits: on the one hand, they are distinguishable from the souls of the dead, and on the other, they are those who have not yet attained the divine nature of gods. In character they are rather tame, yet they sometimes represent something more than a simple personification of a magical rite, a magical property or object. All over Australia, it seems that they were thought of as distinct in form and even when we have sufficient information about them they still appear quite specialized. Among the Arunta we find magical spirits, *Orunchas* and *Iruntarinias*, who are really local genies and who are set apart by their relatively complex nature. In eastern Melanesia spirits are invoked which are not souls of the dead, nor are they all gods, properly speaking. They are spirits which play a considerable role, especially in nature rites: *vui* in the Solomon Islands, *vigona* in Florida, etc. In India, along with the *Devas*, the gods, we have *Pisâkas*, *Yâksasas*, *Râkshasas*, etc., and the whole group, from the moment we have a classification, forms the category of *Asuras*, the main personalities of which include Indra's rival Vrtra and *Namuci*. We all know that Mazdaism considered, on the contrary, that the *Daevâs*, servitors of Ahriman, were the adversaries of Ahura Mazda. Now and then, in these two cases, we come across specialized magical beings. They are evil genies, it is true. Nevertheless, their very names betray the fact that there was never a radical distinction between them and the gods—at least in the beginning. Among the Greeks these magical beings were the δαίμονες, which, as we saw, were similar to the souls of the dead. The specialized nature of these spirits was such that magic was defined in Greek by reference to its relations with demons. There are demons of all kinds, of both sexes, of all shapes and sizes—some are localized on earth, others people the atmosphere. Some are given proper names, although they are all magical. The fate of all the Sxiuoves was to become evil genies and go and live among the *Cercopes*, *Empusae*, *Keres*, etc., as a category of evil spirits. Furthermore, Greek magic showed a marked preference for Jewish angels, particularly the archangels and the same applies to Malayan magic. Eventually all these arch-angels, *archontes*, demons, eons, etc. formed a genuine pantheon of hierarchic magic. This was later inherited by medieval magic, in the same way as the whole of the Far East inherited the magical pantheon of the Hindus. Demons, however, were changed into devils and set up alongside Satan-Lucifer, on whom all magic depended. Nevertheless, in the magic of the Middle Ages and also that of our own times, in places where the old traditions have been preserved, we find that our system has other genies, fairies, sprites, goblins, kobolds, etc.

Magic, however, need not address itself to specialized genies. In fact, the different classes of spirits we have just mentioned were not always exclusively magical in nature. And once they have become magical, this does not mean they do not relinquish the religious role: we do not consider Hell as a magical idea. On the other hand, there are countries where the functions of gods and demons are not distinguishable from each other. This is the case all over North America, where Algonquian *manitous* constantly change from one to the other. The same occurs in eastern Melanesia where the *tindalo* behave in the same way. In Assyria, there are whole series of demons which may or may not be gods. In the scriptures their names usually have divine affixes. The main ones include the *Igigi* and the *Anunnaki*, whose identity is still somewhat mystifying. All in all, demoniacal activities are not at all incompatible with those of the gods. Moreover, the existence of specialized demons does not mean that magic cannot make use of other spirits, endowing them, at least for the time being, with a demoniacal function. And we find gods—and in Christian magic, saints—who crop up as spiritual auxiliaries of the magicians. In India, the gods play their part even in black magic, in spite of the degree of specialization which has developed there, and they play essential roles in all other magical ritual. In countries which have undergone Hindu influence, Malaysia and Câmpa (Cambodia), the entire Brahman pantheon figures in their magic. As for the Greek magical texts, they first of all mention a host of Egyptian gods, either by their Egyptian or their Greek names, as well as Assyrian and Persian gods, Iahwé (Jehovah) and the whole gamut of Jewish angels and prophets— they are all gods who were outside Greek culture. However, they also used the 'high gods', in their form, referring to them by their Greek names, Zeus, Apollo, Aesculapius, even associating them with their particular localities. In Europe, the Virgin, Christ and the saints are the only spirits which appear in most of the spells and particularly in the mythical charms.

Personal representations in magic have presented a sufficient consistency for myths to have grown up. Mythical charms, of the kind just mentioned, depend on myths pertaining to magic. There are others which explain the origin of magical tradition, of sympathetic relations, ritual, etc. However, while magic may have its myths, these are only rudimentary and very specific in nature, dealing only with things rather than with spiritual beings. Magic has little poetry. We do not find many stories about its demons. Demons are like soldiers in an army, they are troops, *ganas*, bands of hunters or cavalcades; they lack any real individuality. This applies even more to the gods which have become involved in magic. They are stripped of personality leaving—if we may be allowed to express it this way—their myths on the doorstep. Magic is not interested in them as individuals, but as wielders of properties, powers whether generic or specific in nature. Moreover, they may be transformed to suit a magician's purpose, and are often reduced to mere names. In the same way that spells can invoke demons, so the gods may also end up as nothing more than mere incantations.

The fact that magic has made use of gods shows that it has been able to take advantage of the obligatory beliefs of society. It is because gods were believed in that magic used them for their own ends. But demons, along with gods and the souls of the dead, are objects of collective representations, which are often obligatory and sanctioned, at least in ritual. This is the reason why they became magical forces. In fact, each magical system would be able to draw up a limited catalogue of spirits, limited in type if not in number. This hypothetical and theoretical limitation provides us with the first hint of the collective character of our demoniacal representations. Secondly, demons may be named in the same way as gods. Since they are normally used for all kinds of purposes, the multiplicity of their services has given them a kind of individuality, and each is, individually, the subject of a tradition. Furthermore, commonly held beliefs in the magical power of a spirit being always presuppose that the spirit has given the public proof of its powers in the form of miracles or successful actions. A collective experience, or at least a collective illusion, is necessary before a demon, properly speaking, can be created. Finally, let us remember that most magical spirits are exclusively presented through ritual and tradition. Their existence is proved only after the growth of the belief which endows them with respect. Therefore, in the same way that impersonal representations of magic seem to have no reality outside collective traditional beliefs—beliefs which are held in common by a group concerned—in our view, personal representations are also collective. We even feel that the proposition will be more acceptable in this case.

4 General Observations

The vague, multiform character of the spirit powers with which magicians have to deal is also a feature of magic as a whole. At first sight, the facts we have collected together may seem very disparate. Some tend to merge magic with technology and science, while others assimilate it to religion. In fact, it should be placed somewhere between the two, but it cannot be defined by its aims, processes or its ideas. Up to the present, our studies have shown that the subject is even more ambiguous, more indeterminate than ever. It resembles non-religious techniques in its practical aspects, in the automatic nature of so many of its actions, in the false air of experiment inherent in some of its important notions. But it is very different from techniques when we come to consider special agencies, spirit intermediaries and cult activities. Here it has more in common with religion because of the elements it has borrowed from this sphere. There are almost no religious rites which lack their magical equivalent. Magic has even developed the idea of orthodoxy as we see in the διαβολαί, those magical accusations dealing with impure rites in Greco-Egyptian magic. However, apart from the antipathy which magic shows towards religion and vice versa (an antipathy, moreover, which is neither universal nor constant), its incoherence and the important role played by pure fancy make it a far cry from the image we have learnt to associate with religion.

Nonetheless, the unity of the whole magical system now stands out with greater clarity. This is the first gain to be made from our incursions into the subject and our long discussions. We have reason to believe that magic does from a real whole. Magicians share the same characteristics, and the effects of their magical performances—in spite of an infinite diversity—always betray much in common. Very different processes can be associated together as complex types and ceremonies. Quite disparate notions fuse and harmonize without the whole losing anything of its incoherent and dislocated aspects. The parts do, in fact, form a whole.

At the same time the whole adds up to much more than the number of its parts. The different elements which we have dealt with consecutively are, in fact, present simultaneously. Although our analysis has abstracted them they are very intimately and necessarily combined in the whole. We considered it sufficient to define magicians and magical representations by stating that the former are the agents of magical rites, while the latter are those representations which correspond to them—we considered them together in relation to magical rites. We are not in the least surprised that our fore-runners have preferred to consider magic solely as a series of actions. We might also have defined magical elements in relation to the magician. Each presupposes the other. There is no such thing as an inactive, honorary magician. To qualify as a magician you must make magic; conversely, anyone who makes magic is, at least for the moment, a magician. There are part-time magicians who revert immediately to their status of layman as soon as the rite is accomplished. As for representations, they have no life outside ritual. Most of them offer little of theoretical interest to the magician and he rarely formulates them. They have solely a practical interest, and as far as magic is concerned they are expressed almost entirely through actions. The people who first reduced them to systems were philosophers, not magicians. It was esoteric philosophy which promulgated a theory of magical representation. Magic itself did not even attempt to codify its demonology. In Christian Europe, as well as in India, it was religion which classified demons. Outside ritual, demons exist only in fairy tales and church dogma. In magic, therefore, we have no pure representations and magical mythology is embryonic and thin. While in religion ritual and its like on the one hand, and myths and dogmas on the other, have real autonomy, the constituents of magic are by their very nature inseparable.

Magic is a living mass, formless and inorganic, and its vital parts have neither a fixed position nor a fixed function. They merge confusedly together. The very important distinction between representation and rite sometimes disappears altogether until we are left with the mere utterance of a representation which thereby becomes the rite: the *venenum veneno vincitur* is an incantation. The spirits which the sorcerer possesses or which possess the sorcerer may become confused with his soul or his magical powers. Spirits and sorcerers sometimes have the same name. The energy or force behind the rite—that of the spirit and the magician—is usually one and the same thing. The normal condition of magic is one involving an almost total confusion of powers and roles. As a result, one of its constituent features may disappear without the nature of the whole changing. There are magical rites which fail to correspond to any conscious idea. The action of spell-binding is a case in point, as well as many imprecations. Conversely, there are cases where representations absorb the ritual, as in genealogical charms, where the utterance of natures and causes constitutes the rite. In sum, the functions of magic are not specialized. Magical life is not compartmentalized like religion. It has not led to the growth of any autonomous institutions like sacrifice and priesthood. And, since magical facts cannot be divided up into categories, we have been forced to think in terms of abstract elements. Magic is everywhere in a diffuse state. In each case we are confronted with a whole, which, as we have pointed out, is more than the sum of its parts. In this way we have shown that magic as a whole has an objective reality—that it is *some* thing. But what kind of thing is it?

We have already gone beyond the bound of our provisional definition by establishing that the diverse elements of magic are created and qualified by the collectivity. This is our second, noteworthy advance. The magician often qualifies professionally through being a member of an association of magicians. In the final count, however, he always receives this quality from society itself. His actions are ritualistic, repeated according to the dictates of tradition. As for representations, some are borrowed from other spheres of social life: the idea of spirit beings, for example. Further research will be required, involving religion directly, if we are to find out whether this idea is the result of individual experience or not. Other representations are not derived from the observations or reflections of individuals, nor does their application allow any individual initiative, since they are remedies and formulas which are imposed by tradition and which are used quite uncritically.

While elements of a magical system are collective in nature, can the same be said for the whole? In other words, is there some basic aspect of magic which is not the object of representations or the fruit of collective activities? Is it not, in fact, absurd or even contradictory to suppose that magic could ever be, in essence, a collective phenomenon, when, in order to compare it with religion, we have chosen, from among all its characteristics, those which set it apart from the regular life of society? We have seen that it is practised by individuals, that it is mysterious, isolated, furtive, scattered and broken up, and, finally, that it is arbitrary and voluntary in nature. Magic is as anti-social as it can be, if by 'social' we primarily imply obligation and coercion. Is it social in the sense of being, like a crime, secret, illegitimate and forbidden? This is not quite true, at least not exclusively so, since magic is not exactly the reverse side of religion, in the way that crime is the reverse side of the law. It must be social in the manner of a special function of society. But in what way should we think of it? How are we to conceive the idea of a collective phenomenon, where individuals would remain so perfectly independent of each other?

There are two types of special functions in society which we have already mentioned in relation to magic. They are science and technology on the one hand, and religion on the other. Is magic a kind of universal art or possibly a class of phenomena analogous to religion? In art or science the principles and methods of action are elaborated collectively and transmitted by tradition. It is for these reasons that science and the arts can be called collective phenomena. Moreover, both art and science satisfy common needs. But, given these facts, each individual is able to act on his own. Using his own common sense, he goes from one element to the next and thence to their application. He is free: he may even start again at the beginning, adapting or rectifying, according to his technique or skill, at any stage, all at his own risk. Nothing can take away his control. Now, if magic were of the same order as science or technology, the difficulties we previously observed would no longer exist, since science and technology are not collective in every single essential aspect, and, while they may have social functions and society is their beneficiary and their vehicle, their sole promoters are individuals. But it is difficult to assimilate to magic the sciences or arts, since its manifestations can be described without once encountering similar creative or critical faculties among its individual practitioners.

It only remains now to compare magic with religion; and here we are faced with formidable difficulties. We still uphold, in fact, that religion in all its aspects is essentially a collective phenomenon. Everything is done by the group or under pressure from the group. Beliefs and practices, by their very nature, are obligatory. In analysing a rite which we took as a type—that is, sacrifice—we established that society was present and immanent everywhere; that society itself was the real actor in the ceremonial drama. We even went so far as to maintain that the sacred objects of sacrifice were social things, *par excellence*. Religious life, like sacrifice, permits no individual initiative, and invention is admitted only under the form of revelation. The individual feels constantly subordinate to forces which are outside his power—forces which incite him to action. If we are able to demonstrate that within the field of magic there are similar powers to those existing in religion, we shall have shown that magic has the same collective character as religion. All that will then remain to be done will be to show how these collective forces are produced—in face of the isolation which magicians insist on—and we shall thereby conclude that these individuals have merely appropriated to themselves the collective forces of society.

chapter four

An Analysis and Explanation
of Magic

Thus we have gradually reduced our study of magic to the pursuit of collective forces which are active in both magic and religion. Indeed, we believe that once these collective forces are found, we will have an explanation for both the whole of magic and its parts. In fact, we should never forget that magic is continuous in nature and that its elements, which are extremely interdependent, frequently seem to be little more than different reflections of the same thing. Actions and representations are inseparable to such an extent that magic could be called a *practical idea*. Taking into account the monotony of its actions, the limited variety in its representations, the sameness which is found throughout the history of civilization, we might also assume magic to be a practical idea of the utmost simplicity. We should, therefore, expect that the collective forces involved would be far from complex and that the methods thought up by the magician to use them would be far from complicated.

We shall try to determine these forces by first posing the problem as to the kind of beliefs of which magic has been the object, and then analysing the idea of magical efficacity.

1 Belief

Magic, by definition, is believed. Since, however, we cannot separate the various aspects of magic and since they frequently merge, they cannot be the object of very clear-cut beliefs. They are all, at one and the same time, the object of the same affirmation. This includes not only the magician's power and the value of the ritual, but also the totality of, and the principles behind, magic. Just as the whole of magic is more real than its parts, so a belief in magic is generally more deeply rooted than beliefs in its separate parts. Magic, like religion, is viewed as a totality; either you believe in it all, or you do not. This can be verified in those cases where the reality of magic has been questioned. When this kind of debate first arose, at the beginning of the Middle Ages, then again in the seventeenth century and today where it is carried on obscurely, we find that discussion always turns on a single point. Agobard of Lyons, for example, was concerned only with people who brought about bad weather. Later it was the fact of impotence being caused by spells, or the aerial flights of Diana's suite. Balthasar Bekker in *De Betoverde wereld* (Leeuwarden, 1691) was concerned solely with the existence of demons and the devil. And in our times it is astral bodies, apparitions, the reality of the fourth dimension. But in all cases conclusions are immediately generalized, and a belief in a single case of magic implies the belief in all possible cases. Conversely one negative instance topples the whole edifice; magic itself then comes under suspicion. We have examples of obstinate credulity and deeply rooted faith crumbling before a single experience.

What is the nature of these magical beliefs? Have they anything in common with scientific ones? The latter are *a posteriori* beliefs, constantly submitted to the scrutiny of individuals and dependent solely on rational evidence. Does the same hold for magic? Evidently not. We have one case, extraordinary though it may seem, of the Catholic Church upholding belief in magic as a dogma, and maintaining it with sanctions. In general, these beliefs are automatically diffused throughout society. They are separated from their origins. In this sense, magical beliefs are not so very different from scientific beliefs, since every society has its science, equally diffuse, whose principles have sometimes been transformed into religious dogmas. But while all science, even the most traditional, is always conceived as being positive and experimental, magic is *a priori* a belief. Magical beliefs, of course, derive from experience: nobody seeks out a magician unless he believes in him; a remedy is tried only if the person has confidence in it. Even in our own days, spirits do not admit unbelievers into their midst. Their presence is believed to render their activities null and void.

Magic has such authority that a contrary experience does not, on the whole, destroy a person's belief. In fact, it escapes all control. Even the most unfavourable facts can be turned to magic's advantage, since they can always be held to be the work of counter-magic or to result from an error in performance of the ritual. In general, they are seen to stem from the fact that the necessary conditions of the rite were not fulfilled. Cross-examination during the trial of the magician Jean Michel, who was burned alive in Bourges, 1623, showed that this poor man—a carpenter by profession—spent his whole life carrying out experiments which always failed. Once he almost achieved his aim but, overcome by fear, he ran away. Among the Cherokee, the failure of a magical rite, far from undermining the people's confidence in the sorcerer, merely endowed him with greater authority, since his offices were indispensable to counteract the terrible effect of the powers, which might return to harm the clumsy individual who had unleashed them without taking the correct precautions. This happens in all magical experiments. Fortuitous coincidences are accepted as normal facts and all contradictory evidence is denied.

Nonetheless, there has always been a pressing urge to support magical beliefs by providing precise, dated and localized proof. In cases where a whole literature on the subject exists—in China and medieval Europe, for example—it will be found that an identical recital of facts is repeated *ad infinitum* from text to text. They are traditional proofs, anecdotal magical tales which are used to bolster magical beliefs, and they are pretty much the same the world over. In all this, we are not dealing with any conscious sophistry, but rather with exclusive prepossession. Traditional proof is sufficient and magical stories are believed in the same way as myths. Even in those cases where magical tales are jokes, there are very few examples of any turning out badly. Belief in magic, then, *a priori* is quasi-obligatory and exactly analogous to belief in religion.

These beliefs hold for the sorcerer as well as for society. But how is it possible for a sorcerer to believe in magic, when he must constantly come face to face with the true nature of his methods and their results? Here we must confront the serious problem of fraud and simulation in magic.

In order to deal with this question, let us take the case of the Australian sorcerers. Of all magical practitioners, there are few who seem so firmly convinced of the efficacy of their ritual. Yet keen observers have attested that the sorcerer has never—nor believed he has ever—seen any automatic effects of his actions in rites practised under normal conditions. Let us look at the methods of black magic. In Australia they may be reduced to three main types and are practised either concurrently or separately in the various tribes. The first type—and the most widespread—is sympathetic magic proper, whereby an object which is believed to be part of a person, or to represent him, is destroyed. These objects may include left-over food, organic remains, footprints, images. It is impossible to imagine that the magician ever believed, by virtue of any experiment, that he was really killing somebody by burning bits of food mixed with wax or fat, or by piercing an image. Our suspicion that the illusion is only a partial one is confirmed by the rite mentioned by B. Spencer and F. J. Gillen, involving first the piercing of an object representing the soul of the victim, and secondly the throwing of the object in the direction of his dwelling. The second type of ritual, practised primarily by the southern, central and western tribes, involves the removal of the fatty parts of a person's liver. It is believed that the sorcerer approaches his sleeping victim, cuts open his side with a stone knife, removes the fat and closes the wound before leaving the spot. The victim dies slowly, unaware of anything untoward having happened. Quite clearly this rite could never have actually been carried out. A third type, practised in the north and central regions is known as 'pointing the bone'. The sorcerer is believed to hit his victim with some fatal substance. In fact, however, the weapon is not even thrown in some of the instances cited by W. E. Roth. In others, it was thrown but from such a distance that it would be impossible to imagine that it ever arrived or transmitted, through contact, the fatal wound. Often it is not even seen to leave the magician's hand and certainly never seen to arrive immediately after having been thrown. Although many of these rites would never have been completely realized and although the effectiveness of many others can never have been proved, they are nevertheless in current usage, as has been shown by the best witnesses and by the existence of numerous objects signifying the tools of their magic. It must be accepted that the sorcerer sincerely, though willingly, believes his gestures to be a reality and the beginnings of an action to be complete surgical operations. The ritual preliminaries, the gravity of each move, the intensity of the dangers undergone (the rite involves approaching an enemy's camp where, if found, he would be killed on sight) and the seriousness of the whole performance reveals a genuine will to believe in it. However, it would be very hard indeed to imagine an Australian magician opening up the liver of his victim without causing instant death.

However, along with this 'will to believe', there is plenty of proof of actual belief. The best ethnographers confirm that the magician deeply believes in the success of his sympathetic magic. In assuming cataleptic and nervous states, he may truly fall prey to all kinds of illusions. At all events, while the sorcerer may have only a mitigated confidence in his own rites and is doubtless aware that the so-called magical poisoned arrows, which he removes from the bodies of people suffering from rheumatism, are only pebbles taken from his mouth, the same sorcerer still has recourse to another medicine man when he himself falls ill. And he will either be cured or allow himself to die, according to whether his doctor condemns him to death or pretends to save him. Thus, while there are some people who do not even see the poisoned arrows depart, there are others who see them arriving at their destination. They arrive as whirlwinds, flames cleaving their way through the air, or as small pebbles, which the medicine man extracts from his body, yet the patient knows full well that they have not been removed from his body. The minimal sincerity which the magician can be accredited with is, at any rate, that he does believe in the magic of others.

This holds true for systems of magic outside Australia. In Catholic Europe we have at least one case where the confessions of a witch were not forced out as a result of the judge's inquisition. At the beginning of the Middle Ages the canonical judge and the theologian refused to accept the existence of the flights of witches in Diana's suite. But the witches, victims of their delusions, continued to boast about them, to their own detriment, finally imposing their fantasies on the Church. These untutored, yet intelligent people, like witches everywhere, easily misled and prey to nervousness, held their beliefs with a sincerity and tenacity which was incredibly strong.

Nonetheless, we are forced to conclude that there has always been a certain degree of simulation among these people. We are in no doubt that magical facts need constant encouragement and that even the sincerest delusions of the magician have always been self-imposed to some degree. A. W. Howitt relates, with reference to the pieces of quartz which the Murring sorcerers draw from their mouths—the initiating spirit packs them into their bodies—that one of the sorcerers told him: 'I know all about it. I know where they come from'. We have other confessions, no less cynical.

In cases such as these, we are not dealing with simple matters of fraud. In general, the magician's simulations are of the same nature as those observed in nervous conditions. As a result, it is both voluntary and involuntary at the same time. Even when it starts off as a self-imposed state, the simulation recedes into the background and we end up with perfect hallucinatory states. The magician then becomes his own dupe, in the same way as an actor when he forgets that he is playing a role. Nevertheless, we must ask why he pretends like this. Here we must be careful not to confuse true magicians with those charlatans who turn up at fairs, or Brahman jugglers who brag to us about spirits. The magician pretends because pretence is demanded of him, because people seek him out and beseech him to act. He is not a free agent. He is forced to play either a role demanded by tradition or one which comes up to his client's expectations. It may appear that the magician vaunts his prowess of his own free will, but in most cases he is irresistibly tempted by public credulity. Spencer and Gillen found a host of people among the Arunta who declared they had taken part in magical excursions, known as *kurdaitchas*, where the liver fat of an enemy is 'removed'. A good third of the warriors have, as a result, had their toes disjointed, since this is a condition of the accomplishment of the rite. And the whole tribe declared they had seen, really seen with their own eyes, the *kurdaitchas* roaming their camps. In fact, most of them were loath to remain outside all this atmosphere of 'fanfaronade' and adventure. The wish to 'encourage belief' was mutual and general throughout the social group, since credulity was universal. In cases of this kind, the magician cannot be branded as an individual working on his own for his own benefit. He is a kind of official, vested by society with authority, and it is incumbent upon the society to believe in him. We have already pointed out that the magician is appointed by society and initiated by a restricted group of magicians to whom society has delegated its power to create magicians. Quite naturally he assumes the spirit of his function, the gravity of a magistrate. He is serious about it because he is taken seriously, and he is taken seriously because people have need of him.

Thus, what a magician believes and what the public believes are two sides of the same coin. The former is a reflection of the latter, since the pretences of the magician would not be possible without public credulity. It is this belief which the magician shares with the rest, which means that neither his sleights of hand nor his failures will raise any doubts as to the genuineness of magic itself. And he himself must possess that minimal degree of faith—a belief in the magic of others, when he is a spectator or patient. Generally speaking, while he does not see the causes at work, he does see the effects they produce. Indeed, his faith is sincere in so far as it corresponds to the faith of the whole group. Magic is believed and not perceived. It is a condition of the collective soul, a condition which is confirmed and verified by its results. Yet it remains mysterious even for the magician. Magic as a whole is, therefore, an object *a priori* of belief, a belief which is unanimous and collective. It is the nature of this belief that permits magicians to cross the gulf which separates facts from their conclusions.

'Belief' implies the adherence of all men to an idea, and consequently to a state of feeling, an act of will, and at the same time a phenomenon of ideation. We are, therefore, correct in assuming that this collective belief in magic brings us face to face with a unanimous sentiment and a unanimous will found in the community or, in other words, precisely those collective representations which we have been looking for. Some people, no doubt, will query the theory of belief we are putting forward and object that a single scientific error, naturally of an intellectual order, through its diffusion, may give birth to beliefs which in time become unanimous, beliefs which we can find no reason for not calling collective, yet which do not derive from collective forces, examples of such beliefs might include canonical beliefs in geocentrism and the four elements. We must now turn our attention to finding out whether magic depends entirely on ideas of this kind, ideas which cease to be doubted simply because they have become universal.

2 An Analysis of Ideological Explanations Concerning the Effectiveness of Ritual

In examining magical representation, we have already considered those ideas by which magicians and theorists explain the efficacy of magical beliefs. These are: 1, sympathetic formulas; 2, the notion of property; 3, the notion of demons. We have already seen that these ideas are far from simple and continually overlap with each other. We shall now show how none of these ideas, by themselves, has ever been sufficient to justify a magician's belief. If we analyse magical ritual in order to reveal the practical application of these different notions, we shall always find that there is something left over, a residue, which the magician himself is also aware of.

Of course, no magician, and no anthropologist either, has ever attempted to reduce the whole of magic to one or other of these notions. This should put us on our guard against any theory which attempts to explain magical beliefs in these terms. We should also point out that, while magical facts do form a unique category of facts, they usually depend on a single principle, which is alone capable of justifying these beliefs, of which they are the object. While it is true that each of these representations corresponds to a certain type of rite, the whole ritual ensemble must correspond to another representation which is quite general in nature. In order to determine what this may be, let us find out to what extent each of the notions enumerated above fail to explain fully the rites with which it is especially associated.

1. We hold that sympathetic formulas (like produces like; the part represents the whole; the opposite acts on its opposite) will not be sufficient to represent the totality of a rite of sympathetic magic. The remaining elements are not negligible. We shall consider only those sympathetic rites for which we have a complete description. The following ritual related by R. H. Codrington (*The Melanesians*, Oxford, 1891, pp. 200, 201) gives a fairly exact idea of their working:

> In Florida the *manengghe vigona*, when a calm was wanted, tied together the leaves appropriate to his *vigona* and hid them in the hollow of a tree where water was, calling upon the *vigona* spirit with the proper charm. This process would bring down rain to make the calm. If sunshine was required he tied the appropriate leaves and creeper-vines to the end of a bamboo, and held them over a fire. He fanned the fire with a song to give *mana* to the fire, and the fire give mana to the leaves. Then he climbed a tree and fastened the bamboo to the topmost branch; as the wind blew about the flexible bamboo the *mana* was cast abroad and the sun shone out.

We have used this only as an example of a concrete illustration,

since sympathetic rites are generally bound up in a complex con-
textual situation. For this reason, we must conclude that the
symbols themselves are not sufficient to constitute a magical rite.
In fact, while a magician, such as an alchemist, sincerely imagines
that his sympathetic practices are intelligible, he still expresses
astonishment at the extent of the accretions accumulating around
what was abstractly conceived to be the schema of the ritual. 'Why
is it?', writes one alchemist, called the Christian, 'that there are so
many books and evocations to demons? Why all this fabrication of
furnaces and machinery when everything is so simple and so easy to
understand?' Yet all the paraphernalia which surprised our Christian is not without its use. It is an expression of the fact that, along
with the idea of sympathy, we also have the idea of the unleash-
ing of power on the one hand and the magical milieu on the other.

There are quite a few indications of this notion of a power
present during rites. First of all, there are sacrifices, which appear to
have no other purpose than the creation of usable forces. We have
already seen that this was one of the attributes of religious sacrifice.
The same applies to prayers, invocations, evocations, etc., and
also to negative rites, taboos, fasting, etc., which are a burden on the
sorcerer or his client or sometimes on both, or indeed on their
families, rites and ritual precautions which mark at the same time
the presence and the fleeting nature of these forces. We should also
take into account the powers belonging to the magician himself,
powers which he carries with him, and the invocation of which is
always at least possible. As for the sympathetic rite itself, we have
already shown that the mere fact of its being ritualistic implies that it
will necessarily produce, in turn, its own special forces. Magicians
have always been conscious of this, in fact. In the Melanesian rite
quoted above we saw how *mana* came out of the leaves and rose up to
the sky. In Assyrian ritual, also mentioned above, *mâmit* is produced.
Let us now consider a sympathetic rite in one of our so-called
primitive societies, one which lacks mystical doctrines and where
society still exists in the magical state. According to Frazer, the
law of sympathy functions regularly and on its own in these societies.
We are immediately aware not only of the presence of forces but
of their movements. Among the Arunta a sympathetic rite performed on an adulterous woman is thought to work the following
way. An evil power, known as *arungquiltha* is, in effect, created.
A stone-soul is charged with it (the image is used to fool the person's

soul and persuade it to come to the rite as if it were still in its own natural body). The evil power is further activated by gestures which simulate the killing of the woman. It is this power which is finally thrown in the direction of the camp where the woman has been abducted. This rite provides an example of a situation where the sympathetic image is not even causal, since it is not the image which is thrown but the charm which the magician has just fabricated.

This is not the whole story. In the same case we find that, apart from the making of the image—where the soul is said to reside for a temporary period only—the rite also involves a collection of additional images which had previously been medicated—spirit stones, needles—and given their power well before the rite. Moreover, the ritual is performed at a secret spot, a spot validated by myth. We shall be bold enough to generalize from this example and conclude that sympathetic rites never occur in the same way as any ordinary act. They must take place in a special milieu, a milieu constructed by all the requisite magical conditions and practices. The milieu may be closed off by boundaries of taboos, and there are both entry and exit rites. Everything which enters this milieu belongs to the same nature as the sympathetic rite, or is endowed with it. The general tenor of all gestures and words becomes affected by it. The explanation of certain magical rites by reference to the laws of sympathy leaves us, therefore, with a twofold residue.

Does this apply in every possible case? We are inclined to believe that this residue is an essential part of magical rites. In fact, once all trace of mystery disappears we enter the realms of science and technology. This is precisely what our Christian alchemist was trying to say. When he discovers that alchemy refuses to be scientific, he bids it become religious. If prayers are required, it is preferable that they be made to god rather than to the devil. This is to admit that alchemy and, as an extension, magic depend essentially on mystical powers. In cases where sympathetic formulas appear to be functioning on their own, we still find, accompanying the minimal form which every rite has, the presence of a minimal mysterious force—this is a matter of definition. Added to this, there is also the force of active property, without which, as we have already pointed out, there would be no way of properly conceiving a sympathetic rite. Moreover, we are still inclined to believe that so-called simple rites have been incompletely observed or have been incompletely performed, or else they have suffered a contraction which makes them useless as examples. As for the really simple rites, involving laws of sympathy, we shall call them sympathetic taboos. It is precisely these rites which best reveal the presence, the instability and the violence of those hidden spirit forces, the intervention of which, to our way of thinking, makes for the effectiveness of magical rites.

We have just seen that sympathetic formulas are never the complete formula of a magical rite. We could produce facts to show that, even when they are present in the clearest fashion, they are still only accessory elements. This is true of the practices of alchemists. They have always formally stated that their operations are rational deductions based on scientific laws. These laws, as we have seen, involve the notion of sympathy: one is the whole, the whole is in one, nature triumphs over nature. There are also special pairs of sympathies and antipathies, a whole complex system of symbols through which they order their operations—signs which are astrological, cosmological, sacrificial, verbal, etc. All this paraphernalia acts as a kind of fancy-dress for their techniques; it cannot even be considered as the imaginary principles of a false science. At the beginning of their books, prefacing each chapter of their manuals, we find an exposition of their doctrines. The rest of the text, however, does not fit the introduction. The philosophical idea is prefixed in the manner of a caption, a heading or allegory, like the man of copper who was changed into gold by sacrifice. This quasi-scientific study can, in fact, be reduced to myths, myths which on occasion provide incantations. The same applies to their experimental precepts. There are algebraical formulas and schemas of actual operations, diagrams of apparatuses which once served a purpose but have since been transformed into unintelligible magical signs, no longer used for performing experiments; they are no more than power-inducing charms. Apart from such principles and formulas, of whose worth we are now perfectly aware, alchemy is an empirical study. It involves such activities as boiling, melting, vaporizing substances whose properties and reactions are understood empirically or traditionally. The term scientific is only a fancy title. The same once applied to medicine. Marcellus of Bordeaux headed a good number of chapters with such phrases as '*Remedia physica et rationabilia diversa de experimentis*'. But immediately afterwards we read a sentence like this: '*Ad corcum carmen.*

In lamella stagnea scribes et ad collum suspendes haec', etc. (Marcellus, xxi, 2).

We may well conclude from the above that the formulas of sympathetic magic are not the laws of magical rites nor even those of sympathetic rites. They are but the abstract expression of very general notions which we have found to be diffused throughout magic. They are nothing more. Sympathy is the route along which magical powers pass: it does not provide magical power itself. In a magical rite the residue after the sympathetic formulas have been abstracted provides us with the essential elements of magic. If we take another example and look at those rites which Sidney Hartland described as sympathetic ritual by contact, the kind of spells by which a sorcerer dries up a woman's milk by kissing the child, we should like to stress the fact that popular beliefs in spells such as these attach less importance to the idea of contact than to the evil eye, or the magical powers of the sorcerer or evil fairy.

2. We also claim that the idea of magical properties in themselves, even in cases where they predominate, cannot explain a belief in magical facts.

In the first place, the idea of properties is not the only element involved. The use of objects which have properties is usually prescribed by ritual. There are rules about the way they should be collected. Conditions of time, place, means, intention and so on have to be fulfilled wherever possible. A plant must be picked from the side of a river, by a crossroad, at the full moon, using two special fingers, with the left hand, approaching from the right, after going first here and then there, without thinking this or that, etc. And there are similar prescriptions for the collection of metals, animal products, etc. Finally, there are regulations regarding their use, the time, place, quantities involved, without going into the sometimes vast array of accessory rites which accompany them and which allow the utilization of their properties and the application of their sympathetic mechanisms. There are systems of magic— in India, for example—where every element involved in a magical rite, either as a secondary charm or an active substance, must be medicated or sacrificed beforehand.

In the second place, magical attributes are not conceived as being naturally, absolutely and specifically contained in the object to which they are attached; they are always relatively extrinsic and conferred.

Sometimes this is achieved through ritual: sacrifice, blessing, bringing into contact with holy or polluted objects or other general sympathetic procedures. In other cases, the existence of the said property may be validated by myth, but even then it is considered accidental or acquired: such and such a plant grew in the footprints of Christ or Medea; aconite flourished in the teeth of Echidna; Donnar's broom and the plant of the celestial eagle are magical objects whose qualities are not naturally inherent in the nut tree of the Hindu plant.

In general, magical properties, even an object's specific property, are considered to derive from characteristics which, from all the evidence, can only be regarded as secondary. This applies, for example, to the accidental shape of stones which resemble taros, pig's testicles and pebbles with holes in them. It is the colour of a lizard's head, in India, or a lump of lead, river foam, etc., which explains the connexion they have with evil substances. Other characteristics include an object's toughness, its name, its rarity value, its mysterious presence in a particular spot (a meteorite, prehistoric stone axes) or the circumstances of its discovery. The magical properties of an object derive from a kind of convention, a convention which plays the role of a sort of embryonic myth or rite. Anything which possesses magical properties, by its very nature, is a form of rite.

In the third place, the idea of properties plays such a relatively insignificant role in magic that it is always confused with very general ideas of power and nature. While people's idea of a desired effect is a very precise one, the idea of special qualities and their immediate action is always quite obscure. On the other hand, we do find very clearly in magic the idea of objects possessing infinite powers: salt, blood, saliva, coral, iron, crystals, precious metals, the mountain ash, the birch, the sacred fig, camphor, incense, tobacco, etc., all incorporate general magical forces susceptible of application or specific use. Moreover, the magician's attitude towards these properties is very commonly general and vague in the extreme. In India things have either a good or bad augury. Those with a good augury are the ones containing *urjas* (power), *tejas* (brightness), *varcas* (lustre, vitality), etc. For the Greeks and the moderns we also find holy, sacred and mysterious objects, which bring either good or bad luck. In sum, magic seeks philosophers' stones, cure-all, panaceas, divine waters.

Let us return to the alchemists, who developed a theory of magical powers based on sympathetic operations. These operations were, for them, forms, εἴδη of a generic nature, of nature, φύσις. If we break up the εἴδη we find the φύσις. However, as we have already stated, they were not concerned with an abstract conception of nature, but conceived it as a kind of essence, οὐσία, or force δύναμις, with vague spiritual properties, which nonetheless have a corporeal basis. Thus, once we are confronted with the idea of nature we also have the idea of force. Nature and force in their most abstract conception, are represented as a kind of impersonal soul, a power distinct from the objects themselves, yet one which is intimately bound up with them, understood though unconsciously. Before leaving the alchemists, we should remember that while the notion of spirit was found to be linked to the idea of properties, the converse is also true. Property and force are two inseparable terms. Property and spirit are often intermingled. The virtues of the *pietra buccata* come from the *follettino rosso* lodged there.

The idea of properties is also bound up with the idea of magical milieu. This is defined by negative or positive prescriptions involved in the use of things which we have already discussed. Finally, this representation is perfectly expressed in a certain number of traditions which imply that contact with a certain object immediately transports us into a magical world: magic wands, magic mirrors, eggs laid on Good Friday. Nevertheless, the residue left behind from the idea of properties, when we try to analyse magical ritual as the product and sum of these properties, is much smaller than it was in the case of sympathetic formulas. This is because the idea of property already partly expresses the idea of force and magical causality.

3. Demonological theory seems better able to account for rites in which demons figure. It even seems to provide a total explanation for rites which involve an appeal or a command addressed to a demon. We could, at a pinch, extend the idea to the whole of magic, although it would be difficult to explain the basic nature of demoniacal rites through the notions of sympathy or magical properties. On the one hand, there are no magical rites which do not betray the presence of personal spirits to some extent, even if they are not necessarily specifically mentioned. On the other hand, the theory implies that magic has to operate within a special milieu, everything taking

place in a world peopled by demons, or more precisely under such conditions that the presence of demons would be feasible. Finally, this theory clearly brings out one of the essential characters of magical causality—its involvement with spirits. Nevertheless, the theory has its drawbacks.

Demons cover only one part of the forces involved in a magical action, even in demoniacal rites. The idea of spirit beings is not a sufficient representation of anonymous general forces which are the basis of a magician's power, the strength behind his words and actions, the power of his looks and intentions, spells and death. This idea of a vague power, then, which we have covered as the residue of the other series of representations, is the total representation of a magical rite. It is so essential that magic has never been able to express its totality, in the form of demons, in a demoniacal rite. Something else must always be left over to explain at least the theurgical action of the rite on the demons, who possibly may be independent, but are not free agents. On the other hand, if the idea of spirits explains how a magician is able to act at a distance and how the ritual is multiple, it cannot explain either the existence of the ritual or its special features—sympathetic actions, magical substances, ritual prescriptions, private languages, etc. In fact, although demonological theory may suffice as an analysis of part of the residue remaining from other formulas, it is only explaining a *part* and it therefore also leaves a residue—consisting of everything which the other theories almost succeeded in explaining. Thus, in any demoniacal rite the idea of spirits is necessarily accompanied by an impersonal notion of efficacious power.

We may ask whether the idea of power does not itself derive from the idea of spirits. This is a hypothesis which nobody has so far maintained. Nevertheless, it is a logical possibility in a strictly animist theory. A first objection would be that a spirit, in magic, is not, of necessity, an active being. All exorcizing ritual, curative spells and those charms we call origin charms have no other function than to put to flight a spirit whose name, history and activities are pointed out to them. The spirit here is in no way the cornerstone of the rite; it represents simply the object of the rite.

Finally, we should take care not to exaggerate the importance of the idea of persons, even within this class of demoniacal representations. We have said that there are demons who amounted to nothing outside those properties and rites which they so imperfectly personify.

In describing them, little else is involved other than the idea of an influence and the passing on of effects. They are ἀπορροίαι, effluvia. Even the names of Hindu demons show to what a limited extent they ever attained any individuality: *siddhas* (those who have obtained power) *vidyâdhâras* (bearers of learning), the names of 'Prince Siddhi, Prince Shakti' (power) have persisted in Moslem Malay magic. Algonquin *manitous* are also quite impersonal. This fact also comes out in the frequent vagueness as to the number and the names of the demons involved. They usually form a body of troops, a host of anonymous beings (mobs, *ganas*), often called by all kinds of collective names. We query even whether these classes of demons ever involved real people at all—apart from the souls of the dead, who are themselves rarely identified, and the gods.

We not only hold that the notion of spirit power does not derive from the notion of magical spirit, but we have reason to believe that the latter derives from the former. The idea of spirit power, in fact, leads us to the idea of spirit. We find that the Assyrian *mâmit*, the Algonquin *manitou* and the Iroquois *orenda* may all be called 'spiritual', without losing any of their characteristics of general power. On the other hand, is it not a reasonable supposition to imagine that the idea of the magical spirit is the sum of two notions: that of the spirit and that of magical power, the latter not necessarily to be considered as an attribute of the first? Proof of this may be found in the fact that, among the dense crowd of spirits with which society peoples its universe, there are only a limited few that are recognized—through experience, so to speak—as powerful beings and hence involved in magic. This may explain the tendency to bring gods into the system, particularly foreign gods or rejected ones, gods who are, by definition, powerful beings.

Although we were first inclined to favour the animist explanation of magical beliefs over all other theories, we have now noticeably departed from the common animist hypothesis, in that we consider the idea of spiritual force to have preceded the idea of the soul, at least as far as magic is concerned.

To sum up, the various explanations which can be brought forward as motives for beliefs in magical acts leave a residue, which we must now try to describe, in the same way as we described the various elements of magic. And we have reason to believe that it will be here that we shall find the real basis of these beliefs.

We have thus come nearer to determining this further element which magic superimposes on its impersonal notions and its ideas of spirits. At this stage, we hold that it is an element which is superior to these two orders of ideas, and one from which—if it is presented—the others are merely derivative.

It is a complex notion, involving first of all the idea of power, or as it has been rather better described, 'magical potential'. It is the idea of a force of which the force of the magician, of the ritual and of the spirit are merely different expressions, in accordance with the elements of magic. The fact is that none of these elements acts as such, but does so precisely inasmuch as it is endowed, either by convention or by special rites, with this character of being a force, and not a mechanical force, but a magical one. The idea of magical force is moreover, from this point of view, quite comparable to our notion of mechanical force. In the same way as we call force the cause of apparent movements so magical force is properly the cause of magical effects: illness and death, happiness and health, etc.

This idea also includes the notion of a milieu, where the powers in question exist. In this mysterious milieu, things no longer happen in the way they do in our world of the senses. Distance does not prevent contact. Desires and images can be immediately realized. It is the spiritual world and the world of the spirits at the same time. Since everything is spiritual, anything may become a spirit. Yet although this power is illimitable and the world transcendental, things happen according to laws, those inevitable relations existing between things, relations between signs and words and the represented objects, laws of sympathy in general, laws of properties which are susceptible to being codified into a system of classifications of the same type as those which have been studied in *Année Sociologique*. The ideas of force and milieu are inseparable, coinciding in an absolute sense. They are expressed at the same time and through the same means. In fact ritual forms, those dispositions aimed at creating magical forces, are also the same as those which create the milieu and circumscribe it before, during or after the ceremony. If our analysis is exact, therefore, we shall find—at the basis of magic—a representation which is singularly ambiguous and quite outside our adult European understanding.

It has been through the discursive processes of similar individual judgments that the science of religion has so far attempted to explain magic. In fact, the theory of sympathetic magic depends on analogical reasoning or—which amounts to much the same—the association of ideas. Demonological theory refers to individual experiences of consciousness and of dreams. The representation of properties is usually conceived as resulting from experience, from analogical reasoning or from scientific error. This composite idea of force and milieu, on the other hand, avoids these rigid and abstract categories, which our language and reasoning impose. From the point of view of an individual's intellectualist psychology, it would be an absurdity. Let us see whether a non-intellectualist psychology of man as a community may not admit and explain the existence of this idea.

3 Mana

A similar notion exists, in fact, in a certain number of societies. By a logical reversal the fact that it exists, is named and is already relatively differentiated in two of our ethnic groups—which we shall use as special examples—provides confirmation of our analysis.

The idea is that found in Melanesia under the name of *mana*. Nowhere else is it so clearly evident and it has fortunately been admirably observed and described by Codrington (*The Melanesians*, p. 119 *et seq.*, p. 191 *et seq.*, etc.). The word *mana* is common to all Melanesian languages proper and also to the majority of Polynesian languages. *Mana* is not simply a force, a being, it is also an action, a quality, a state. In other terms the word is a noun, an adjective and a verb. One says of an object that it *is mana*, in order to refer to this quality; in this case the word acts as a kind of adjective (it cannot be said of a man). People say that a being, a spirit, a man, a stone or a rite *has mana*, 'the *mana* to do such and such a thing'. The word *mana* is employed in many different conjugations—it can be used to mean 'to have mana', 'to give mana', etc. On the whole, the word covers a host of ideas which we would designate by phrases such as a sorcerer's power, the magical quality of an object, a magical object, to be magical, to possess magical powers, to be under a spell, to act magically. The single word embraces a whole series of notions which, as we have seen, are inter-related, but which we have always represented as separate concepts. It reveals to us what has seemed to be a fundamental feature of magic—the confusion between actor, rite and object.

The idea of *mana* is one of those troublesome notions which we had thought to have discarded; we therefore experience difficulty in grasping it. It is obscure and vague, yet the use to which it is put is curiously definite. It is abstract and general, yet quite concrete. Its primitive nature—that is, its complexity and confusion—resists any attempt at a logical analysis, and we must remain content to describe the phenomenon. According to Codrington, it invades all magical and religious rites, all magical and religious spirits, the totality of persons and things involved in the totality of ritual. It is really *mana* which gives things and people value, not only magical religious values, but social value as well. An individual's social status depends directly on the strength of his *mana*, and this applies particularly to roles in secret societies. The importance and inviolability of property taboos depend on the *mana* of the individual who imposes them. Wealth is believed to be the result of *mana*. On some islands *mana* is the word for money.

The idea of *mana* consists of a series of fluid notions which merge into each other. At different times it may be a quality, a substance or an activity. First *mana* is a quality. It is something which possesses the thing called *mana*, not the thing itself. It is described as being 'powerful' or 'heavy'. At Saa it is 'hot', at Tanna it is something strange, indelible, resistant, extraordinary. Secondly *mana* is a thing, a substance, an essence that can be handled yet also independent. That is why it may only be handled by individuals who possess *mana* during a *mana* action, that is, by qualified individuals during the course of a rite. By its nature it is transmissible, contagious: *mana* may be communicated from a harvest stone to other stones through contact. It is represented as a material body. It may be heard and seen, leaving objects where it has dwelt. *Mana* makes a noise in the leaves, flies away like a cloud or flame. It can be specialized: there is *mana* to make people wealthy and *mana* used to kill. Generic forms of *mana* may be defined even more narrowly. In the Banks Islands there is a special kind of *mana*, the *talamatai*, for certain methods of making incantations, and another for casting spells over the traces of an individual. Thirdly *mana* is a force, more especially the force of spirit beings, that is to say, the souls of ancestors and nature spirits. It is *mana* which creates magical objects. However, it is not indiscriminately inherent in all spirits. Nature spirits are essentially endowed with *mana*, but all the souls of the dead are not. *Tindalos* are active spirits—the souls of dead chiefs, for the most part family heads, and more particularly those in whom *mana* has manifested itself either during their lifetime or through the performance of miracles after their death. Only these merit the name of powerful spirits, the others being lost among a multitude of impotent shades.

Once again we have an example of the fact that while all demons are spirits, not all spirits are demons. The idea of *mana*, then, is not to be confused with the idea of spirit. They are closely linked, yet remain profoundly separate. Consequently, there is no possibility of explaining (at least in Melanesia) demonology, and hence magic, through animism alone. Take the following as an example. In Florida, when a man is ill the sickness is explained by the fact that *mana* has him in its grasp. This *mana* belongs to a *tindalo* who is himself associated with a magician (*manekisu*—endowed with *mana*) who has the same *mana* or the *mana* to act on it, which amounts to the same thing. On the other hand, the *tindalo* is also associated with a plant. There are certain plant species attached to different kinds of *tindalos* which, through their *mana*, cause certain illnesses. The *tindalo* concerned is discovered by the following means. The leaves of different species of plants are collected and rubbed between the fingers one by one, the one which contains the *mana* of the illness afflicting the sick person is recognized by a special rustling sound. Now they can confidently call in the *tindalo*, or the *mane kisu* who possesses the *mana* of the *tindalo*, that is, the individual who is related to the spirit and who is alone empowered to remove the *mana* from the patient and bring about his cure. Here, in fact, the *mana* is separable from the *tindalo* since it is found not only in the *tindalo* itself, but also in the sick person, the leaves and the magician too. *Mana*, therefore, exists and functions independently. It remains an impersonal force, alongside the personal spirit. The *tindalo* contains *mana* but is not *mana* itself. Note, in passing, that this *mana* circulates within a classificatory category and that the things which act upon one another are encompassed within this category.

Mana, however, need not be the power possessed by a spirit. It may be the force of a non-spiritual object, such as a stone for making taros grow or for rendering sows fertile, or a plant which brings rain. But it is a spiritual force in so far as it does not work mechanically and can produce its effects from a distance. *Mana* is the magician's force. The names of those specialists who perform magic are almost everywhere composed from the word: *peimana*, *gismana*, *mane kisu*, etc. *Mana* is the power of a rite. The word *mana* is even applied to magical formulas. However, the rite is not only endowed with *mana*, it may be *mana* itself. It is because the magician and rite possess *mana* that they are able to act upon spirits with *mana*, evoke them, give them orders, possess them. Therefore, when a magician has a personal *tindalo*, the *mana* which he uses to act upon his *tindalo* is not really different from the *mana* which makes the *tindalo* function. While there is an infinity of *tindalos*, we have come to believe that the different *manas* are but one and the same power, not fixed in any way but simply shared out among beings, men or spirits, objects, events, etc.

We could extend still further the meaning of this word and maintain that *mana* is power, *par excellence*, the genuine effectiveness of things which corroborates their practical actions without annihilating them. This is what causes the net to bring in a good catch, makes the house solid and keeps the canoe sailing smoothly. In the farms it is fertility; in medicine it is either health or death. On an arrow it is the substance which kills and, in this case, it is represented by a piece of bone from a dead man which is incorporated in the arrow shaft. And it is a fact that European experts have shown the Melanesian poisoned arrow to be simply a magically medicated arrow—the arrow with *mana*. However, they are believed to be poisoned, but it is clear that it is the *mana* and not the arrow point to which they attribute the actual effectiveness of the arrow. It is the same in the case of demons—again *mana* appears to be distinct from the *tindalo*, working like a quality attached to an object, without prejudicing its other qualities, in other words, like something superimposed on another. This extraneous substance is invisible, marvellous, spiritual—in fact, it is the spirit which contains all efficacy and all life. It cannot be experienced, since it truly absorbs all experience. The rite adds it to things, and it is of the same nature as the rite. Codrington thought he could call it the supernatural, but then he more correctly says that it is only supernatural '*in a way*', that is to say, that *mana* is both supernatural and natural, since it is spread throughout the tangible world where it is both heterogeneous and ever immanent.

This heterogeneity is always apparent and sometimes manifested in action. *Mana* is separate from the common world of mortals. It is the object of a reverence which may amount to a taboo. We might add that all taboo objects must contain *mana* and that many *mana* objects are taboo. As we have mentioned, these include the *mana* of a property owner or the *tindalo* which endows the property taboo with power. There is even reason to believe as well that the place where spells are made, the stones where *tindalos* dwell—places and objects with *mana*—are taboo. The *mana* of a spirit-dwelling stone will affect any person who walks over the stone or whose shadow crosses it.

Mana is, therefore, seen to be something both mysterious and separate. In sum, *mana* is first of all an action of a certain kind, that is, a spiritual action that works at a distance and between sympathetic beings. It is also a kind of ether, imponderable, communicable, which spreads of its own accord. *Mana* is also a milieu, or more exactly functions as a milieu, which in itself is *mana*. It is a kind of internal, special world where everything happens as if *mana* alone were involved. It is the *mana* of the magician which works through the *mana* of the rite on the *mana* of the *tindalo*, and which sets other *manas* in motion and so forth and so on. In its actions and reactions there are no other forces involved apart from *mana*. It is produced in a closed circuit, in which everything is *mana* and which is itself *mana*, if we may so express it.

The same idea crops up in places outside Melanesia. We find certain indications of it in a number of societies where further research would not fail to uncover it completely. First and foremost, it is widespread among speakers of other Malayan-Polynesian languages. Among the Straits Malays, it is known by a term of Arabic origin with a Semitic root, which has a somewhat more restricted sense—*kramât* (W. W. Skeat's transliteration) from *hrm* which means sacred. Things, places, moments, animals, spirits, men, sorcerers are *kramât* or have *kramât*; and it is the forces of *kramât* which are active. To the north, in French Indo-China, the Ba-hnars express a similar idea to *mana*, when they say that the witch is a *deng* person, who has *deng*, who can *deng* things. They apparently speculate endlessly on the notion of *deng*. At the other extreme of the dispersal of Malayan-Polynesian languages, in Madagascar, we have the term *hasina*—of unknown etymology—which refers at one and the same time to the quality of certain things, an attribute of some beings—animals, men and, in particular, the queen—as well as the ritual controlling these qualities. The queen was *masina*, she had *masina* and the tribute presented to her, together with the oath sworn in her name, was *hasina*. We are convinced that a closer analysis of New Zealand magic where *mana* plays a role—and even of the Dayaks, where the medicine man is called *manang*—would provide similar conclusions to the studies carried out in Melanesia.

The Malayan-Polynesian world can claim no monopoly of these concepts. In North America we find the same in certain regions. Among the Huron (Iroquois) it is called by the name *orenda*. Other Iroquois seem to have called it by a term which has the same root. J. N. B. Hewitt, a Huron by birth, and a distinguished ethnographer, has given a valuable description—a description rather than an analysis, since the *orenda* is no easier to explain than *mana*. (*American Anthropologist*, 1902, new series, 4, i, pp. 32–46.)

The idea is too general and too vague, too concrete, covering so many things and so many obscure qualities that it is only with difficulty that we can begin to understand it. *Orenda* is power, mystical power. There is nothing in nature, particularly anything endowed with life, which is without *orenda*. Gods, spirits, men, animals are all endowed with *orenda*. Natural phenomena, such as storms, are produced by the *orenda* of the spirits of these phenomena. The fortunate hunter is one whose *orenda* has defeated the *orenda* of his prey. The *orenda* of animals hard to catch is said to be intelligent and cunning. Everywhere among the *Huron* there are examples of struggles between different *orenda*—in the same way as we found struggles between different *manas* in Melanesia. And the *orenda*, like *mana*, is distinct from the objects to which it is attached, to such a degree that it can be exhaled, thrown into the air—the spirit which brings thunderstorms throws up his *orenda* in the form of clouds. *Orenda* is also the sound of an object. Animals crying, birds singing, rustling trees, the blowing of the wind—all are expression of *orenda*. In the same way the voice of the magician is *orenda*. The orenda of things is like an incantation. In fact, the name Huron, when uttered aloud, is none other than *orenda*. In addition, *orenda* means, in its original sense, prayers or chants. This meaning of the word is confirmed by the terms which correspond to it in other Iroquois dialects. But although incantations are *orenda, par excellence*, Hewitt expressly informs us that all ritual is *orenda*, and this aspect again reminds us of *mana. Orenda* is, above all, the power of the shaman. He is called *rareñdiowa'ne*, somebody whose *oɾenda* is great and powerful. A prophet or diviner, *ratreñ'dats* or *hatreñdotha* is someone who habitually exhales or effuses his *orenda*, and in this way learns the secrets of the future. It is *orenda* which is magic's active ingredient. Everyone who practises magic is said to be possessed by *orenda*, activated by it rather than by virtue of any physical properties. This is what gives power to spells, amulets and fetishes, mascots, lucky charms and, if you like, medicines. It is particularly active in black magic. All magic, therefore, derives from *orenda*.

We have some hints that lead us to believe that *orenda* works through a system of symbolic classification. The cricket is called the *ripener of the corn*, because it sings on hot days, that is its *orenda* which brings warmth to make the corn grow; 'the rabbit "sings", and by barking the underbrush at a suitable height, indicates the depth to which the snow must fall. Thus his *orenda* controlled the snow.' The hare is the totem animal of a clan in one of the Huron phratries, and this clan has the power to bring fog and snowfalls. It is, therefore, the *orenda* which unites the various classificatory terms which include the hare, the totemic clan, fog and snow on the one hand, and on the other, the cricket, heat and corn. In this classification it plays the role of middle term. These texts also give us an idea of the way the Iroquois represent causality. For them, the cause, *par excellence*, is the voice. To sum up, *orenda* is not material power, it is not the soul, nor an individual spirit, nor is it strength nor force. Hewitt establishes, in fact, that there are other terms to express these various notions and he correctly defines *orenda* as a 'hypothetic potence or potentiality to do or effect results mystically.'

The famous concept of *manitou* found among the Algonquins and particularly among the Ojibway is basically the same as our Melanesian *mana*. The manitou, according to Father Thavenet—the author of an excellent French-Algonquin dictionary still in manuscript—refers, in fact, not to a spirit, but to a whole species of spirits, forces and qualities (Tesa, *Studi del Thavenet*, Pisa, 1881, p. 17).

'It means being, substance, the state of being animate and it is quite clear that to a certain extent all beings with souls are manitous. But it particularly refers to all beings which still have no common name, which are not familiar. A woman who came across a salamander said she was afraid, thinking it to be a manitou. The people laughed at her and told her the name of the animal. Trade beads are manitou's scales, and *cloth*— wonderful as it is—is said to be the skin of a manitou. A

manitou is an individual who performs extraordinary feats—
a shaman is a manitou. Plants have manitous. A sorcerer who
uses the tooth of a rattlesnake will say that it is a manitou;
when it is found to have no power to kill, he says that it no
longer has manitou.'

According to Hewitt, among the Sioux the terms *mahopa*, *Xube*
(Omaha), *wakan* (Dakota) also mean magical power and magical
qualities.

Among the Shoshone the word *pokunt* generally (according to
Hewitt) has the same value, the same meaning as manitou has among
the Algonquin. J. W. Fewkes, who has recorded material on the
Hopi or Moki, states that among the Pueblo in general the same
ideas are at the bottom of all magical and religious ritual. J. Mooney
appears to be referring to the same kind of thing among the Kiowa.

The term *naual* in Mexico and Central America seems to us to
correspond to the same idea. Here it is so persistent and widespread
that it has been applied to all systems of religion and magic by
referring to the whole as nagualism. *Naual* is a totem, usually an
individual totem. However, it is more than this: it covers a much
wider category. The sorcerer is *naual*—he is a *naulli*; *naual* is his
power to transform himself, his metamorphosis and his incarnation.
It is, therefore, clear that an individual totem, an animal species
which is associated with the person from birth, is but one form of
naual. Etymologically, according to Seler, the word means 'secret
science', and all its different meanings and derivatives are connected
with its original meaning of 'thought' and 'spirit'. In nauahtl texts
the word expresses the idea of being hidden, enveloped, disguised.
Thus, it seems to us that the term contains the idea of a separate,
mysterious, spiritual power, which is exactly what is implied in
magic.

In Australia, we find a concept of a similar kind. Here it is
clearly restricted to magical activities, and more particularly to
black magic. The Perth tribes give it the name of *boolya*. In New
South Wales, the tribes use the word *koochie* to describe an evil
spirit, personal or impersonal evil influences, and it probably has the
same extension. Again we find the *arungquiltha* of the Arunta. This
'evil' power, which is conjured up in rites of sympathetic magic, is
at one and the same time a force and an object in itself which is
described in myths and to which they attribute a specific origin.

The fact that our examples of this idea of 'power-milieu' are few and far between, should not lead us into any doubt about the universality of the institution. We are, in fact, poorly informed on these kinds of facts. The Iroquois have been known for three centuries, but it was only a year ago that our attention was drawn to *orenda*. And indeed, the idea may well exist without having been expressed: people have no more need to express ideas like these than they need to formulate the rules of their grammar. In magic, as in religion and linguistics, unconscious ideas are at work. In some cases, the people have not become fully aware of these ideas. In others, they have passed the intellectual stage in which they normally function. At all events, they have not been able to provide an adequate expression of the phenomena. Some people have removed the earlier, mystical aspects of their old beliefs in magical power. Magic then becomes quasi-scientific in nature; this happened in Greece. Others have formulated entire dogmas, mythologies and demonologies and, as a result, have reduced everything that they found to be vague and obscure in their magical representations to mythical terms, which—at least on the surface—replaced the idea of magical power with the devil, demons or metaphysical entities. This was the case in India. They have thereby brought about the almost total disappearance of the idea.

Nevertheless, we find glimpses of it. In India it crops up under such separate notions as brightness, glory, force, destruction, fate, remedy, the qualities of plants. And the basic idea of Hindu pantheism, contained in *brahman*, seems to us to be profoundly connected with it. It even appears to perpetuate the idea—as long as we can hypothetically assume that the Vedic *brahman*, the Upanishads and Hindu philosophy are one and the same. Briefly, we believe that there has been a veritable metempsychosis of ideas. Although we can grasp its beginning and end, we are ignorant of the intermediary stages. In both the most ancient and more modern of the Vedic texts, the word *bráhman* (neuter) means prayer, formula, rite, the magic or religious power of the rite. The magician or priest is called by the name of *brahmán* (masculine). Between these two terms there is only sufficient difference to separate the diversity of functions. There is not enough difference to signify any opposition between the two ideas. The brahmanical caste is the caste of the *bráhmanas*, that is men who possess *bráhman*. *Bráhman* is that which activates men and gods, referring particularly to the voice. In addition to these facts, we have certain texts which refer to it as the substance, the core of things (*pratyantam*)—the innermost part; these are all Atharvanic texts, that is, Veda texts of magicians. However, the idea has already begun to be confused with that of the newly introduced god Brahmâ, a masculine word, derived from *Bráhman*. *Bráhman* ritual no longer appears in theosophical texts and we are left with metaphysical *bráhman*. *Bráhman* becomes the active, distinct and immanent principle of the whole universe. Only *bráhman* is real, all else is illusion. As a result, anyone who would enter the bosom of *bráhman* through mystical activities (*yoga*: union) becomes a *yogi*, a *yogicvara*, a *siddha*, that is, one who has gained all magical powers (*siddhi*: obtaining), and in this way, it is said, has placed himself in the position of creating worlds. *Bráhman* is the prime, total, separate, animate and inert spirit of the universe; it is the quintessence. It is also the triple Veda as well as the fourth, that is to say, religion and magic.

In India alone the mystical basis of the idea has survived. In Greece we have little more than its scientific framework. We find it under the concept of φύσις, on which, in the final analysis the alchemists depended, and also in δύναμις, the last resort of astrology, physics and magic. δύναμις is the action of φύσις and φύσις is the action of δύναμις. φύσις can be defined as a kind of material soul, non-individual, transmissible, a kind of unconscious understanding of things. It comes, in fact, very close to the idea of *mana*.

From the foregoing, we feel justified in concluding that a concept, encompassing the idea of magical power, was once found everywhere. It involves the notion of automatic efficacy. At the same time as being a material substance which can be localized, it is also spiritual. It works at a distance and also through a direct connexion, if not by contact. It is mobile and fluid without having to stir itself. It is impersonal and at the same time clothed in personal forms. It is divisible yet whole. Our own ideas about luck and quintessence are but weak survivals of this much richer concept. As we have seen, as well as being a force, it is also a milieu, a world separated from— but still in touch with—the other. In order to explain more clearly how the world of magic is superimposed on the other world without detaching itself from it, we might go further and add that everything happens as if it were part of a fourth spatial dimension. An idea like *mana* expresses, in a way, this occult existence. This image applies so well to magic that modern magicians, confronted with the discovery that geometry had more than three dimensions, took over these speculations to legitimize their own rites and ideas.

All this provides us with an idea of what goes on in magic. It provides us with a necessary concept of a field where ritual occurs, where the magician is active, a place where spirits come alive and where magical effluvia are wafted. It also legitimizes the magician's powers and justifies the need for formal actions, the creative virtue of words, sympathetic connexions and the transfer of properties and influences. Moreover, it explains the presence of spirits and their intervention, since it conceives all magical force as being spiritual force. Finally, it motivates general beliefs in magic, since all magic may be reduced to this idea, once it has shed its outer form. At the same time it further encourages these beliefs, since it is the very idea which animates all the forms assumed by magic.

This concept means that the reality of magic need no longer be brought into question; doubts may even be turned to its advantage. It is an idea which is, in fact, the very condition of magical experimentation and permits the most unfavourable facts to have the benefit of the doubt. Indeed, it is above all criticism. It exists, *a priori*, before all other experience. Properly speaking, it is not a magical representation in the same way as those representations of sympathy, demons and magical properties. It produces magical representations and is a condition of them. It functions as a kind of category, making magical ideas possible in the same way as we have categories which make human ideas possible. The function, which we are attributing to it here, of an unconscious category of understanding, is truly brought out by the facts. We have already pointed out that it was uncommon for it to become part of a people's consciousness and even more uncommon for it to find any expression. The fact is that it is inherent in magic in the same way that Euclid's propositions are inherent in our concepts of space.

Of course, it will be clear that it is a category which does not exist in an individual's understanding in the same way as our categories of time and space. The proof of this lies in the fact that it has been so considerably reduced owing to the progress made by civilization, and that its character changes from society to society and according to the different life styles found in one society. It is present in an individual's consciousness purely as a result of the existence of society, in the same way as ideas of moral value and justice. We are confident that we are dealing with a category of collective thinking.

Our analysis also brings out the fact that *mana* is an idea of the same order as the idea of the sacred. In the first case, the two ideas merge in a number of instances. Notable examples include the idea of manitou among the Algonquins, the *orenda* of the Iroquois and *mana* in Melanesia, which are all magical as well as religious. Further, we have already seen that in Melanesia there is a relationship between the ideas of *mana* and taboo: a certain number of things with *mana* were taboo, but only *mana* objects could be taboo. The same holds good for the Algonquin: all gods are manitous, but all manitous are not gods. As a result, we find that not only is the idea of *mana* more general than that of the sacred, but that the sacred is inherent in the notion of *mana* and derives from it. It would probably be fair to say that the sacred is a species of the genus *mana*. In this way, as far as magical ritual is concerned we would not only have found more than the idea of the sacred, but we would find the substratum of the whole.

However, let us return to the dilemma of our preface. Either magic is a social phenomenon and the idea of the sacred is also a social phenomenon, or magic is *not* a social phenomenon and neither is the idea of the sacred. Without wishing to enter into any discussion on the nature of the sacred itself, we should like to make a number of points in order to stress the social aspect of both magic and *mana*. The quality of *mana*—and of the sacred—appertains to things which are given a very definite position in society, often to the extent of their being considered to exist outside the normal world and normal practices. These things play a very considerable role in magic; they provide, in fact, its living forces.

Magical beings and magical things notably include the souls of the dead and everything associated with death. Witness the eminently magical character of the universal practice of evoking the dead. Witness the qualities attributed to the 'hand of death', any contact which makes objects invisible in the same way as death does—and a thousand other facts. The dead themselves are the focus of funeral ceremonies and, sometimes, ancestor cults, which mark so clearly the different status of the dead in relation to the living. You may object that magic only concerns people who die violent deaths, particularly criminals. This is further proof of the point we wish to make here. Persons may be the object of beliefs and rites which convert them into beings of quite a different sort, not only from the living but also from the rest of the dead. Nevertheless, on the whole, all dead people, both bodies and spirits, form a separate world from that of the living, a world from which the magician derives his powers to kill, his black magic.

The same applies to women. It is because they have a special social status that they are thought to play important magical roles, considered to be sorceresses, attributed with special powers. Female attributes are qualitatively different from men's and give them specific powers. Menstruation, the mysterious actions of sex and childbirth are signs of those qualities ascribed to them. Society— the society of men—nourishes strong social sentiments toward women, which the latter both respect and share. From this stems their different—inferior—legal status and particularly their different religious status. It is precisely these factors which determine their role in magic, and in magic they enjoy a status the opposite to that which they hold in religion. Women are a constant source of malignant influence. *Nirrtir hi strî*, 'woman is death', say the old brahmanical texts (*Maitrayânî samhitâ*, 1, 10, 11). They bring misery and witchcraft. They possess the evil eye. It is for this reason that they play a more important role in magic than in religion, although they are, in fact, far less active than men would have us believe.

These two examples show how the magical value of persons or things results from the relative position they occupy within society or in relation to society. The two separate notions of magical virtue and social position coincide in so far as one depends on the other. Basically in magic it is always a matter of the respective values recognized by society. These values do not depend, in fact, on the intrinsic qualities of a thing or a person, but on the status or rank attributed to them by all-powerful public opinion, by its prejudices. They are social facts not experimental facts. And this is excellently demonstrated by the magical power of words and the fact that very often the magical power of an object derives from its name. Consequently, since they depend on dialects and languages, the values in question are tribal or national ones. In the same way, things and beings and actions are organized hierarchically, controlling one another, and magical actions are produced according to this ordering: they go from the magician to a class of spirits, from this class to another, and so on, until they achieve their effect. The reason why we like Hewitt's phrase 'magic potence', which he uses to describe *mana* and *orenda* is because it brings out precisely the presence of a kind of magical potential, and it is, in fact, exactly the idea we have been describing. What we call the relative position or respective value of things could also be called a difference in potential, since it is due to such differences that they are able to affect one another. It is not enough to say that the quality of *mana* is attributed to certain things because of the relative position they hold in society. We must add that the idea of *mana* is none other than the idea of these relative values and the idea of these differences in potential. Here we come face to face with the whole idea on which magic is founded, in fact with magic itself. It goes without saying that ideas like this have no *raison d'être* outside society, that they are absurd as far as pure reason is concerned and that they derive purely and simply from the functioning of collective life.

We in no way wish to imply that this hierarchy of ideas, dominated by *mana*, is the product of multiple, artificial contracts between individuals either magicians or ordinary laymen, ideas which traditionally came to be accepted in the name of reason, in spite of being crammed with initial errors. On the contrary, we hold that magic, along with religion, has to deal with sentiments. To be more precise, we would affirm, using the abstruse language of modern theology, that magic, like religion, is a game, involving 'value judgments', expressive aphorisms which attribute different qualities to different objects entering the system. However, these value judgments are not the work of individual spirits. They are the expression of social sentiments which are formed—sometimes inexorably and universally, sometimes fortuitously—with regard to certain things, chosen for the most part in an arbitrary fashion: plants, animals, occupations, sex, heavenly bodies, the elements, physical phenomena, landscape patterns, materials, etc. The idea of man, like the idea of the sacred, becomes in any final analysis nothing more than a kind of category of collective thinking which is the foundation for our judgments and which imposes a classification on things, separating some, bringing together others, establishing lines of influence or boundaries of isolation.

4 Collective States and Collective Forces

We might end here and conclude that magic is a social phenomenon, since we have uncovered the notion of collectivity behind all of its manifestations. However, in its present form, the idea of *mana* still seems to us to be too cut off from social life; there is still something too intellectual about it. We have no clear idea whence it comes, on what foundations it flourished. Therefore, we shall try to dig deeper still, in order to reach those forces, those collective forces, which we claim to have produced magic and of which *mana* is the expression.

In order to do this, let us consider for a moment magical representations and magical practices as judgments. We are justified in doing so, because all kinds of magical representations take the form of judgments, and all kinds of magical operations proceed from judgments, or at least from rational decisions. Take the following examples: the magician conjures up his astral body; clouds are produced by smoking such-and-such a herb; a spirit is moved by the ritual. We shall now see—in a completely dialectical or critical fashion, if you like, to use the useful if obscure language of Kantian philosophy—that judgments like these are explained only in society and through society's intervention.

Are they analytical judgments? We have to ask this question, since both the magician who produces his theory of magic and the anthropologist who does likewise have attempted to reduce them to analytical terms. The magician, they say, reasons from like to like by applying the law of sympathy, thinking in terms of his powers or his auxiliary spirits. The rite causes the spirits to work, by definition. The magician conjures up his astral body because this body is himself. The smoking of the aquatic plant brings a cloud because it is a cloud. However, we have clearly shown that this reduction to analytical terms is quite theoretical and that things really happen otherwise in the magician's mind. His judgments always involve a heterogeneous term, which is irreducible to any logical analysis. This term is force or power, θύσις or *mana*. The idea of magical efficacy is ever present and plays far from an accessory part, since it enjoys the same role which the copula plays in a grammatical clause. It is this which presents the magical idea, gives it being, reality, truth, makes it so powerful.

Let us continue to use the methods of philosophy. Are magical judgments synthetic judgments *a posteriori*? Do their syntheses, on which they depend, exist ready made in an individual's experience? We have found that the experience of our senses has never furnished any proof of a magical judgment. Objective reality has never imposed any proposition—of the kind we formulated above—on the human mind. Obviously you need the eyes of faith to see an astral body, the smoke that brings rain, and (most particularly in this case) an invisible spirit which obeys ritual.

There are others who say that these propositions result from subjective experience, on the part either of individuals concerned in the rite or of the magician. They say that the former see these things happening because they want to and that the latter undergoes hallucinatory states, dreams and ecstasies, in which impossible syntheses become logical. We should not wish to play down the importance of wish-fulfilment and dreams in magic; we are merely leaving this subject aside for the moment. Yet even if we were to admit for a moment that there are two levels of human experience, the merging of which produces magic, we should soon discover—if we were to consider individuals only—that these levels do not coincide as far as spirits are concerned. Imagine for a moment—if you possibly can—the state of mind of a sick Australian aborigine who calls in a sorcerer. Obviously a series of suggestive phenomena takes place in the man's mind and he will either be cured through hope or allow himself to die, convinced that he has been condemned to do so. Beside him the shaman dances, falls into a cataleptic fit, has dreams. His dreams take him up into the other world and when he comes back, deeply affected by his long journey into the world of souls, animals and spirits, he cunningly extracts a small pebble from the patient's body, which he says is the evil spell which has caused the illness. Obviously there are two subjective experiences involved in these facts. And between the dreams of one and the desires of the other there is a discordant factor. Apart from the sleight of hand at the end, the magician makes no effort to make his ideas coincide with the ideas and needs of his client. These two very intense individual states coincide only at the moment of the conjuring trick. At this unique moment a genuine psychological experience takes place, either on the part of the magician—who can hardly be under any delusion at this stage—or on that of the patient. The so-called experience of the magician is no more than an error of perception,

I

which would be unable to answer criticism and consequently be unrepeatable, if it were not sustained by tradition or a permanent act of faith. Individual subjective states, just as poorly adjusted as the ones we have pointed out, cannot in themselves explain the objectivity, the universality and the apodictic nature of magical statements.

All these things are beyond criticism because people do not want to question them. All over the world where magic flourishes, magical judgments existed prior to magical experience. They are the canons of the ritual, the links in the chain of representations. Experiences occur only in order to confirm them and almost never succeed in refuting them. You may object and point out that these judgments are historical or traditional facts, and that at the origin of each rite or myth there was once a real individual experience. However, there is no need to follow up this idea of primary causes since we have already said that magical beliefs are dominated by a universal belief in magic which goes beyond the fields of individual psychology. It is this belief which allows people to objectivize their subjective ideas and generalize individual illusions. Again, it is this belief which gives magical judgments their affirmative, inevitable and absolute character. In brief, while they exist in the minds of individuals, magical judgments, even from the outset, are—as we have pointed out—well nigh perfect, *a priori*, synthetic judgments. The terms are connected before any kind of testing. However, it must be made clear that we have no wish to imply that magic does not demand analysis or testing. We are only saying that it is poorly analytical, poorly experimental and almost entirely *a priori*.

What, then, operates this synthesis? Can it be done by the individual? There has never been, in fact, any need to operate it. Magical judgments arise in the form of prejudice and prescription, and they appear in this way in the minds of individuals. However, let us leave aside this question of fact for a moment. We cannot conceive of any magical judgment which is not the object of a collective confirmation. It must always be supported by at least two persons—the magician performing the rite and the individual who believes in it—or else, as in the case of folk magic, practised by single individuals, the person who teaches the remedy and the one who practises it. This theoretically irreducible pair of individuals in fact forms a society. More usually, however, magic has the support of more extensive groups, whole societies and cultures.

If we have magical judgments we also have a collective synthesis, a unanimous belief—at any given moment—in the truth of a certain idea, the effectiveness of a certain gesture. We obviously do not hold that ideas associated with such syntheses cannot also be associated—or, indeed, are not associated—with an individual consciousness. The idea of dropsy, for example, naturally suggested to Hindu magicians the idea of water. It would be absurd to suppose that all magical thinking avoided the laws of association of ideas. The ideas which form these magical circuits have names and are certainly not contradictory. However, the natural association of ideas simply serves to render magical judgments possible. Magical judgments are far from being a mere collection of images. They are real, imperative precepts, which imply a positive belief in the objectivity of the chain of ideas which they form. As far as the mind of an individual is concerned, there is nothing which requires it to associate—in the categorical way magic does—words, actions or instruments with the desired effects, unless it be experience, and it is precisely this experience which we have just shown to be impotent. A magical judgment is imposed by a kind of convention which establishes, prejudicially, that a symbol will create an object, and a part will create the whole, a word, the event and so on. Actually the essential fact is that the same associations should necessarily be reproduced in the minds of several individuals or rather of a mass of individuals. The universality and the *a priori* nature of magical judgments appear to us to be the sign of their collective origin.

It follows, therefore, that it is only those collective needs, experienced by a whole community, which can persuade all the individuals of this group to operate the same synthesis at the same time. A group's beliefs and faith are the result of everyone's needs and unanimous desires. Magical judgments are the subject of a social consensus, the translation of a social need under the pressure of which an entire series of collective psychological phenomena are let loose. This universal need suggests the objective to the whole group. Between these two terms, we have an infinity of possible middle terms (that is why we have found such an extreme variety of rites employed for the same purpose). Between the two terms we are allowed a degree of choice and we choose what is permitted by tradition or what a famous magician suggests, or we are swept along by the unanimous and sudden decision of the whole community. It is because the result desired by everyone is expressed by everyone, that the means are considered apt to produce the effect. It is because they desired the healing of feverish patients that cold water douches and sympathetic contact with a frog seemed—to those Hindus who sought the help of the Brahmans of the Atharaveda—sufficiently powerful remedies against third- or fourth-degree fever. The whole society suffers from the false images of its dream. The synthesis between cause and effect occurs only in public opinion. If magic is not conceived in this way it will be seen only as a chain of absurdities and errors. We would find it extremely hard to understand its invention, and possibly harder to grasp its diffusion.

Magic should be considered as a system of *a priori* inductions, operating under the pressure of the needs of groups of individuals. Furthermore, we may wonder whether or not a large number of hasty generalizations made by humanity did not derive from similar circumstances, or whether, indeed, magic was not responsible for them. It is even possible that inductive reasoning was first learnt in the school of magic. This is because, if we may hazard a somewhat radical hypothesis concerning individual psychology, it does not appear to us that isolated individuals, or even the human race as a whole, can really reason inductively. They can merely acquire instincts and habits which, in fact, lead to the abolition of all reflection on actions.

However, stripped of all simplistic hypotheses, our arguments will appear even more acute if we remember that all magical affirmations, even the most spiritual of them, depend on a completely universal affirmation of magical power, which is itself contained in that of *mana*. As we have clearly seen this is an idea—both in matter and form—which is collective. There is nothing intellectual or experimental about it except the feeling of society's existence and society's prejudices. This is the idea, or rather the category, which explains logical possibility of magical judgments and avoids condemning them as absurdities. It is a remarkable fact that this obscure idea, which we have had such difficulty in separating from the vague nature of affective states, an idea which is almost untranslatable into abstract terms and which is inconceivable to us, should be precisely that idea which provides believers in magic with clear, rational and, occasionally, scientific support. The idea of *mana*, in so far as it is implied in all kinds of magical propositions, becomes, as a result, an analytical concept. Consider the following proposition:

the smoke given off by aquatic plants brings clouds. If we were to insert, after the subject of the sentence, the word *mana*, we should immediately have the equation—smoke with *mana* = clouds. This idea not only transforms magical judgments into analytical judgments but converts them from *a priori* to *a posteriori* arguments, since the idea dominates and conditions all experience. Thanks to the idea of *mana*, magical dreams not only become rational but they also become confused with reality. It is the faith of the patient in the power of the magician which makes him actually feel the drawing of his illness out of his body.

From all this we hope to have shown that we are far from wishing to replace psychological mysticism with sociological mysticism. First of all, collective needs do not lead to the formulation of instincts, of which we have but one example in sociology—the instinct of sociability, the initial condition of all others. Moreover, we do not recognize one pure collective sentiment. Those collective forces which we are trying to uncover produce manifestations which are always, at least in part, rational and intellectual in nature. Thanks to the idea of *mana*, magic—the domain of wish-fulfilment—is shown to have plenty of rationalism.

Thus, if magic is to exist, society has to be present. We shall now try to show that this is so and to what extent it is so.

It is generally held that prescription and coercion are the sure signs of direct action in society. Magic is not made up of obligatory beliefs and rites; it has shared ideas and voluntary rites. Nor have we found any example of coercion as such. Nevertheless, this does not mean that we have not come across the existence of prescriptions, or at least avoidances, with regard to certain objects and actions, which are observed by the whole society. They do, in fact, exist in magic and probably originated there. They include certain sympathetic taboos and others we might call 'mixed' taboos. For example, a pregnant woman should not see a murderer or a house where someone has died. The Cherokee are continually prey to taboos—not only the patient, but the magician himself, the whole family and all neighbours. As we have seen, these prescriptions constitute genuine negative rites—while they may not be absolutely obligatory they are, at least, observations which have been imposed upon the group. In truth, it is not really society which punishes any infringements. The magical taboos we are dealing with have automatic punishments and are sanctioned by the inevitable consequences which follow their violation. Nevertheless, it is, of course, society which really imposes a belief in these automatic sanctions and which supports them.

Individual negative rites, popular taboos, are not the only prohibition set up by magic. Sometimes, as we have seen, a positive rite is also accompanied by a whole farrago of negative rituals. They include, in particular, the kind of rites performed prior to a ritual ceremony. The magician, or the magician and his patient, refrain from food and sex, and undergo purificatory rites before taking part in the ceremony, showing thereby the incompatibility they feel between the things they have to touch or do and the circumstances of everyday life. They are aware of a kind of resistance; magic is not an easily opened door. Further prescriptions and fears accompany the rites of exit, reflecting the fact that they are leaving the abnormal world they had entered. Moreover, they do not emerge unscathed. Magic, like sacrifice, requires and produces an alteration, a modification in one's state of mind. This is expressed by the gravity of the actions, the changed nature of the voice and even by the use of a special language, the language of spirits and gods. In magic, therefore, negative ritual forms a kind of threshold, where a person is stripped of his individuality and becomes an actor.

In magic, as well as in religion, we find a close correlation between negative rites and positive rites. We hold it reasonable to believe, without having any satisfactory proof, that all positive rites and all positive properties correspond to certain negative rites and negative properties. A taboo on iron, for example, reflects the magical qualities of the blacksmith. No matter how voluntary the positive rite, it is more or less directly connected with a negative rite which is either obligatory or at least believed to be sanctioned by automatic, ineluctable effects. Beings and actions, agents and myths, in magic as well as religion, are all subject to these effects, almost tabooed. The most common magical objects, the more familiar magical beings—the village bone-mender or a horseshoe—all inspire some kind of respect. The simplest magical rite, the most innocent spirit seance, all invoke a sense of awe. There is always a degree of hesitation or inhibition, sometimes produced by the same feeling of repugnance which religion induces. Magic attracts and at the same time repels. At this point, we return to the idea of secrecy and mystery with which magic is imbued and which provides its distinctive features. These are the features we noted when we were seeking to define magic and which now betray those collective forces which create it. Magic has a system of ritual prescriptions which is peculiar to magic itself, a system which, so far from being haphazard, contributes to the characterization of its very nature. Moreover, magic is closely bound up with the whole system of collective taboos, including religious prescriptions, to such an extent that we are never quite sure whether the magical character of an object derives from the taboo or the taboo derives from its magical character. Left-over food is taboo, but it is taboo because people fear the magical use to which it may be put. Magic has a veritable predilection for forbidden things. The curing of illness and misfortune, which are caused by breaking taboos, is one of magic's specialities and in this field it competes with religion as an expiatory agent. Magic uses the violation of these taboos to its own advantage. It makes use of all the detritus which religion taboos —sacrificial remains which ought to be consumed or destroyed, menstrual blood, etc. It is because of this that magic—as we saw in its negative aspects, at least, and there are many of them—is the very creation of the collectivity. Only society can legislate in this way, imposing those prohibitions and sustaining attitudes of repugnance behind which magic shelters.

Although these factors are observable socially, one is led to ask what there is in that theoretical being we call the individual which creates and nourishes such apprehensions. A repeated experience of things which are harmful to the species will only result in providing him with instincts to protect him against these real dangers. However, it is not a question of this: the mind is crowded with chimerical fears which derive solely from the mutual exaltation of individuals as members of a group. In fact, while magical chimeras are universal, the objects of people's fears vary from group to group. The fears themselves are produced by collective agitation, through a kind of involuntary convention, and are transmitted by tradition. They are unique within a given society. One superstition, for example, and one of the most widespread of all, the evil eye, does not occur in Australia nor in Melanesia, and it appears only in the vaguest form in ancient and non-Muslim modern India.

We have now arrived at the conclusion that there are affective states, generators of illusions, to be found at the root of magic, and that these states are not individual, but derive from a mixture of sentiments appertaining to both individuals and society as a whole.

Here we find ourselves in close agreement with a theory advanced by W. Lehmann. Arguing from the point of view of individual psychology, he explains, as we all know, that magic derives from errors of perception, illusions and hallucinations, as well as acute, emotive and subconscious states of expectation, prepossession and excitability: all range from psychological automatism to hypnosis.

We also agree with this writer that the expectations and illusions which are produced are the primary phenomena of magic. Even the most run-of-the-mill rites, which work automatically, are never devoid of emotions, apprehensions and, above all, hope. The magical power of merely desiring something to happen is so clear that a good deal of magic consists of these desires: the evil eye, eulogia, euphemisms, wishes, almost all incantations in fact. On the other hand, we have shown that direction of intent and arbitrary choice play a preponderant role in determining particular rites and magical beliefs and that they derive from exclusive attentiveness and states of monoideism. We see this in the example of an object used in two totally different rites: burning coals of *arka* wood are put out in order to halt a storm (*arka* = lightning), or a branch is spread on the ground to bring sunshine (*arka*). A single idea, at will, may be sent off in two directions without any sense of contradiction. The attention of the magical agents and spectators is usually so intense, and they feel, on the other hand, that the idea is so precious to them that they could not admit that it could be deflected for an instant without causing harm. Any interruption to the rite means a break and spoils its effect. Spirit seances will admit no distraction. One of the most frequent themes in tales of popular witchcraft, and a good example of the value attached to the constant attention required during a rite, is the case of a person who comes to borrow something during a ceremony, particularly during a rite of counter-magic against a witch. An old woman arrives—the witch, of course—begs to borrow some everyday object, and because they listen to her the spell is broken.

We agree with Lehmann, then, that magic produces mental excitation in individuals. Among water diviners, for example, it may develop into a kind of hyperaesthesia. What we deny is that a magician can reach this state of his own free will or that he feels himself to be an isolated being. Behind Moses, who touched the bare rock, stood the whole nation of Israel, and while Moses may have felt some doubts, Israel certainly did not. Behind the village water diviner and his wand we find the anxiety of a whole village, desperate for water. The state of the individual, we consider, is always conditioned by the state of society. An explanation for Lehmann's theory is that the part played by society in modern magic today is almost entirely subconscious. It can exist without being observed, therefore it can be neglected. We should also point out that it is rare, in our own culture, for the remnants of our magical system to be practised by whole groups. However, there is no need to consider these moribund, poorly developed systems as fundamental ones. It is primitive society where we find the most complex and rich phenomena and where we must go in search of facts to explain the origins of magic, facts which are collective in nature. Furthermore, the psychologists' arguments do not invalidate our own, since each time they observe newly formed magical behaviour, they ought to be aware that it always occurs in a sympathetic milieu, in the bosom of a cult group of spiritualists or followers of the occult.

There are societies where participation in magic is the normal thing. Throughout those regions of Malayan-Polynesian languages and culture, there are whole series of very important magical rites—dealing with hunting, fishing, war—which are performed by the whole community. These rituals are normally accompanied by negative rites observed by society as a whole. Among these observances, the most remarkable and the most elaborate involve purity taboos. The strictest chastity is required of a woman while her husband is away hunting, fishing or fighting. Anything which may disturb domestic harmony or village peace, compromises the lives and the success of the absent men. There is a very close solidarity tie between the men and those who remain at home. The fact of this solidarity is borne out by jural institutions, particularly in Madagascar, where we find a special adultery code: in times of peace this domestic crime carries only civil sanctions, but is punishable by death during times of war. Such collective practices, moreover, are not found exclusively in the Malayan-Polynesian world, although they are best preserved there. In many cases their absence in other magical systems should not surprise us since these things are poorly defined, unstable and subject to sudden change. In other places they become sanctioned and eventually absorbed by religion, or they may simply have degenerated haphazardly into popular folk practices performed by single individuals and with no apparent origins. A host of negative sympathetic rites, which are bound up with pastoral and agricultural life and which are of the most intriguingly arbitrary nature, must be relics of similar systems of collective ritual.

These negative observances we have been dealing with show that the rites with which they are involved affect not only the principal actors, but also all their natural associates. They are public activities, supported by mental states which are shared by the community as a whole. A whole social milieu may be affected by the mere fact that a magical act is being performed in one part of it. A circle of impassioned spectators collects around the action being performed. They are brought to a halt, absorbed, hypnotized by the spectacle. They become as much actors as spectators in the magical performance—rather like the chorus in Greek drama. The society as a whole becomes expectant and obsessed by the rite— we find the same feeling in our own culture, particularly among huntsmen, fishermen or gamblers, all well known for their superstitions. The collecting together of this kind of committed group provides a mental atmosphere where erroneous perceptions may flourish and illusions spread like wildfire; miracles occur in this milieu as a matter of course. The members of such communities are experimenters, who have accumulated a myriad opportunities for error. They are in a state of perpetual aberration, where at any moment a chance event will be proclaimed law, a coincidence a rule.

Magical collaboration is not confined to immobility and non-participation. The whole group is sometimes set in motion. The chorus of onlookers is not always content to play a passive role. Beside the negative rites which occur in public magic, we also find public rites of positive magic in Malayan-Polynesian societies. The whole group, unanimously, pursues a single, preconceived aim. Old Madagascar texts tell us that when the men were away on an expedition women had to maintain a constant vigil, keeping the fires going and dancing continually. These positive rites, even less stable than negative ones, have disappeared among the Hovas, although they have lasted in other places. Among the Dayaks, for example, when the men are off head-hunting, women carry around sabres, which they are not allowed to put down and the whole village, including old people and children, must rise at dawn, at the same time as the warriors absent in the jungle. Among the maritime tribes of New Guinea, when the men go hunting, fishing or fighting, the women spend the whole night dancing. Perhaps these facts demonstrate a kind of 'savage telepathy', as Frazer says. But it is an active telepathy. The whole social body comes alive with the same movement. They all become, in a manner of speaking, parts of a machine or, better, spokes of a wheel: the magical round dance, performed and sung, becomes the ideal image of the situation. This image is probably primitive, but certainly still occurs in our own times in the cases here quoted and elsewhere. The rhythmic movement, uniform and continuous, is the immediate expression of a mental state, in which the consciousness of each individual is overwhelmed by a single sentiment, a single hallucinatory idea, a common objective. Each body shares the same passion, each face wears the same mask, each voice utters the same cry. In addition, we have the terrific impression produced by the rhythm of the music and singing. To see all these figures masked with the image of the same desire, to hear all mouths uttering proof of their certainty—everyone is carried away, there is no possibility of resistance, by the convictions of the whole group. All the people are merged in the excitement of the dance. In their feverish agitation they become but one body, one soul. It is then that the corporate social group genuinely manifests itself, because each different cell, each individual is closely merged with that of the next, like the cells which make up an individual organism. In such circumstances—circumstances which in our society can never be realized, even by the most overexcited crowd, though elsewhere they have been found—a feeling of universal consensus may create a reality. All those Dayak women, dancing and carrying sabres, are really at war. Acting in this way, they actually believe in the success of their ritual. Here the laws of group psychology have more meaning than laws of individual psychology. A whole series of normally sequential phenomena—volition, idea, muscular movement, satisfaction of needs—becomes completely simultaneous in this case. It is because society becomes activated that magic works, and it is because of magical beliefs that society becomes activated. We are no longer dealing with isolated individuals each of which, singly, believes in his own magic, but with a whole group which has faith in the group's magic.

However, those phenomena where, in a manner of speaking, social facts are consciously fabricated, are necessarily rare occurrences. Nevertheless, analogous mental states can be produced without society undergoing such a commotion. This is clearly shown in the descriptions we have of rain-making rites among the Pitta-Pitta of central Queensland. In times of drought; the society of sorcerers, together with the head man, perform rites which include the splashing of certain sticks with water. Society is not content to watch this passively, and once the ceremony is over everyone sings in chorus along with the main actors around the edges of a pool. On the warriors' return to camp, each group tries to outdo the other, carrying on throughout the entire day to the accompaniment of a continuous, monotonous chanting. In this kind of rite, society is only partly playing its role. We have a kind of mental and physical division of labour between the actors and spectators: those influencing and those being influenced in the rite. The two groups are completely and naturally interdependent. Although they may get divided and contact cease, a sympathetic connexion continues and produces mental actions and reactions which, despite the separation, are no less intense. Among actors and spectator-participants alike, we find shared ideas, shared illusions, shared wishes, all of which constitute their communal magic.

We may here generalize on these observations. When the people gather round a magician and then he withdraws into his private world, it may seem at this moment that their participation is also withdrawn, but in fact it is more real than ever at this point because it is society's presence which gives him the confidence to become possessed and permits him to come out of this state in order that he may perform his magic. It is the people's impatience that causes the magician to become excited and which at the same time commits him to the group. Society is willing to be hypnotized by any kind of simulation performed by the magician, and he may himself fall the first victim. This kind of feverish attention and the anticipation which results from it are found among all agricultural and pastoral tribes, even hunting tribes, indeed all people who share large continental environments. One only has to consider the terribly urgent economic pressure involved. Mrs Langloh Parker collected a story in central Australia, which admirably describes the spiritual state of a whole tribe, desperately in need of water. It describes how, because of the tribe's anxiety, the sorcerer was forced to perform and how his influence was recognized to the extent that he brought forth a deluge, which he finally had to stop.

While rain-making is a magical act performed partly in public, medical magic is carried out in the family, though it, too, reveals very clearly defined social conditions. Here we have a minimal social group, it is true, but it is an organized social group with a chief member holding both authority and power—the magician—and an embryonic crowd all attentive, imbued with fear and hope, credulity and illusion. The suggestive power of this milieu, as with the others, is unmistakable. In our own times we still find similar states occurring in Malay medical magic in elementary groups of Hindu or Muslim culture. In Borneo, around the Straits, among the Shams of Indo-China, we find today the family, the sorcerer or sorceress and the patient forming a kind of spirit congress during the consultation. Here the application of the remedy is a secondary factor in the operation. In general, it is clear that medical rites are eminently suggestive, not only as far as the patient is concerned (and we are well informed on his state of mind), but also for the other participants who feel the strain and for whom the magician's gestures, sometimes his trances, provide a fascination which moves them to the core of their beings.

From the facts we have just quoted, it is evident that medical ritual has a magical character which would be hard to dispute. It corresponds sufficiently to the definition of a magical rite which we have given. Nevertheless, some of the other rites, particularly those where we found an almost perfect manifestation of social states, have an obligatory and public character which fits poorly with this definition. Does our explanation of magic then no longer hold? Social phenomena, which were going to provide us with an explanation of magic, may be produced during the performance of a rite which is very definitely public, not because they are magical, but because they meet public needs. As a result, they would seem to bear the mark of religiosity and cult. In so doing, we would appear to have explained the collective character of religion and no magic, fallen prey to the logical error of claiming that we can explain one by the other. Having been so careful to separate magic from religion and having stayed constantly within the field of magic, we now find ourselves surreptitiously drawn into religion. However, we can tackle this problem by emphasizing that the facts involved are not exclusively religious. They have certainly not been taken as such by historians and theorists who preceded us when they dealt with the subject, since they have generally categorized them as magical. One thing is certain, and that is that they are basic to magic, and that when performed they actually become, at any rate partially, magic. Indeed, while we may admit that the ritual of the rainmakers is quasi-religious, this does not deny the fact that the principal role is played by an actor, who most certainly generally practises black magic as well.

Let us now turn to those kinds of rites which do not involve a magician but which are performed by all members of a group as a whole. These kinds of rites are only partly religious. While they may have given rise to cults elsewhere, we do not regard them as an organized form of cult in those places we have observed. We find only a kind of religious tone. It is a milieu in which religion may certainly flourish, even if it has not already done so. Moreover, in these rites we find at least two features of magic, secondary though they may be: constraint and direct, automatic efficacy, without the presence of differentiated, spiritual intermediaries. We believe we are justified in claiming that we are really dealing with facts which perpetuate ideas involved in the concept of *mana*. Dayak women, with their war dances, bring into play this synthesis, which constitutes a magical understanding, implying the notion of *mana*. By their dancing, they are joining in the war, and it is a collaboration which is felt, and believed, to be highly effective. As far as these women are concerned, time and space no longer exist; they are on the field of battle. Experimental forms of causal ideas play no role for them; there is only magical causality. Their entire consciousness is absorbed by a feeling of their power, a feeling of the impotence of things, to such an extent that disappointment in the experience can be explained by them only as the work of contrary forces which have the same nature as their own. Their sensibilities are overwhelmed by the awareness of their existence as a group of women and the social role they are playing in relation to the warriors, an awareness which is translated into sentiments about their own power and the relation of this power with that of their menfolk. All we know about their way of thinking fits in perfectly well with our enumeration of the characteristics of *mana*. We could say that the women were prey to a monotheism (which revolves around a similar idea), or that their ideas, intention and action were all functioning according to the *mana* category. Quite the contrary, there is no hint that the spirit of their actions involves any clear notion of the sacred, which is a sure sign of the religious state.

It is true that, in our opinion, *mana* seems no more magical in concept than does religion. However, since it provides for us the matrix for magical facts, since those facts we have described concerning it correspond so well, we feel certain that we are face to face with the rudimentary data of magic. Yet at the same time we are also convinced that they form the rudimentary data of religion. We shall demonstrate elsewhere how both derive from a common source. If, through the study of these facts, we have been able to show that magic springs from affective social states, we are not displeased if we have, at the same time, verified a hypothesis we have already proffered regarding religion.

Facts similar to those we have just interpreted are to be found elsewhere in the world besides the Malayan-Polynesian and Oceanian countries. They are universal. Collective observances providing proof of the magical solidarity of families and groups are also found in Europe. We have observed such phenomena ourselves. For example, in various parts of France, when a man takes a purge his wife takes one too. These facts, however, are merely survivals of forgotten states. They are weak expressions of the existence of real solidarity feelings and thoughts between persons practising these types of rites communally. As for magical groups, they are also universal. There is probably no place in the world where the general public remains unaffected. The kinds of assemblies and the feelings engendered there are perpetuated in the impatient curiosity of people who stand gaping and crowd round charlatans selling quack medicines at fairs. The little we do know of these facts seems to justify the universal application of our conclusions, and we hope that detailed research into a single magical system will one day prove us right. We are ourselves firmly convinced that group sentiments will always be found at the origin of all magical manifestations, whether the magic was borrowed from an earlier religion or an outside religion, or whether they sprang from the world of magic itself.

Throughout the course of history magic has provoked states of collective sentiment, from which it derives stimulus and fresh vigour. The witchcraft epidemics of the Middle Ages provide one of the best examples of the extent to which fantastic social passion can be excited. While the Inquisition certainly burned more innocent people than real witches, it also served to generate them. On everyone's mind was imprinted the idea of magic and this exercised a terrible fascination. With startling swiftness it brought about mass conversions. Moreover, during witch trials, witches sought each other out, brought together and recruited proselytes and acolytes. Such initiative comes only with a sense of group feeling. There must be at least two persons before risking suspect experiments. United, they become aware of a sense of mystery which affords them protection. In an account of the life of the witch Marie-Anne de la Ville—tried and condemned in 1711—we can read how men specialized in the unearthing of buried treasure grouped themselves around her and refurbished their faith through their mutual activities. However, no magical group, however large, is sufficient unto itself. Each time the members are deceived they need to have their optimism rekindled through the faith of new recruits. In this way the magician of Moulins, whom we have already mentioned as the carpenter Jean Michel, found his faith renewed by contact with his judge's belief, and out came his confessions—from the sheer pleasure of speaking magic.

In this way, the magician receives continual encouragement from outside. Magical beliefs which are active in certain corners of our society and which were quite general a century ago, are the most alive, the most real indications of a state of social unrest and social consciousness, in which there floats a whole crowd of vague ideas, hopes and vain fears, giving form to the remnants of the former category of *mana*. In society there is an inexhaustible source of diffuse magic which the magician uses to his own advantage. Everything happens as though society, from a distance, formed a kind of huge magical conclave around him. This is the reason why the magician lives in a kind of specialized atmosphere which follows him everywhere—if we can express ourselves like this. However cut off from the real world he may seem to others, it does not appear the same to him. His individual consciousness is deeply affected by this social sentiment. As a magician he is no longer himself. If he thinks about his condition, he may come to the conclusion that his magical powers are quite separate from him. He merely has access to them or acts as a kind of depository for them. And if he lacks power, his individual knowledge is useless. Prospero is not Ariel's master. He took over his magical power, when he freed him from the tree where he had been imprisoned by the sorceress Sycorax, on certain conditions and for a certain time. When he gives him back to the elements, to nature and the world, he is nothing but an ordinary mortal and may as well burn his books.

Now my charms are all o'erthrown,
And what strength I have's mine own;
Which is most faint . . .

Throughout its existence, magic has never forgotten its social origins. Each of its elements, agents, rites and representations not only perpetuate the memory of this original collective state, but even help in their reproduction in an attenuated form. Every day society, in a manner of speaking, ordains new magicians, experiences rites, listens to fresh tales, which are always the same. In spite of the fact that there are constant interruptions, society's creation of magic is no less continuous. In communal life, these emotions, impressions, impulses are ceaselessly produced and give rise to the idea of *mana*. People's habits are continually disturbed by things which trouble the calm ordering of life: drought, wealth, illness, war, meteors, stones with special shapes, abnormal individuals, etc. At each shock, at each perception of the unusual, society hesitates, searches, waits. Ambroise Paré himself believed in the universal virtues of the Bezoar stone, which the Emperor Rudolph received from the King of Portugal. These are attitudes which turn the abnormal into *mana*, that is, magic or things produced from magic. Moreover, everything magical is effective, because the expectations engender and pursue a hallucinatory reality. We have seen how, in some societies, a patient who is deserted by the magician dies. We have seen him cured through trust and confidence. It is a kind of comfort which a collective, traditional power of suggestion can provide. The world of magic is full of the expectations of successive generations, their tenacious illusions, their hopes in the form of magical formulas. Basically it is nothing more than this, but it is this which give it an objectivity far superior to that which it would have if it were nothing more than a tissue of false individual ideas, an aberrant and primitive science.

However, while we have this basis of social phenomena, it is a remarkable fact that as soon as magic becomes separated from religion, only individual phenomena arise. Having found social phenomena at the basis of magic, which we earlier defined by its individualistic features, it will be convenient to return to this latter aspect now. While it is impossible to understand magic without taking into consideration the magical group, we can, on the other hand, easily grasp how the magical group resolves itself into individuals. In the same way, it is easy to understand how the public and collective needs of a small primitive group ceded later to very general individual needs. It is also easy to grasp the fact that, once definitive suggestions like education and tradition existed, magic was able to live on as an individual phenomenon.

Magical knowledge seems to have been passed on from individual to individual, just as in the teaching of science and techniques. The means of transmitting magical rites among the Cherokee are instructive on this score. There existed a whole body of magical scholarship and schools of magicians. In order to pass on magical knowledge to individuals, magic had to make it intelligible to individuals. Then there developed experimental or dialectical theory which naturally enough neglected the unconscious collective facts. The Greek alchemists and their successors, our modern magicians, tried to deduce it from philosophical principles. Moreover, all magical systems, even the most primitive or popular, justify their remedies by reference to past experience. And magical systems have developed through objective researches and genuine experiences. They have progressively benefited from discoveries which have been both true and false. In this way, the relative role of the collectivity in magic has been whittled down. It diminished because the collectivity banished everything of an irrational or an *a priori* nature. In this way, magic began to approximate to the sciences and finally came to resemble them in so far as it claimed to result from experimental researches and logical deductions made by individuals. In this as well, magic more and more came to resemble technology, which itself responds to the same positive and individual needs. Except for its traditional character, magic has tried to cast off all collective aspects. Everything involving theoretical and practical achievements now becomes the work of individuals, and it is exploited only by individuals.

chapter five

Conclusion

Magic is, therefore, a social phenomenon. It only remains for us to show what place it holds among the other social phenomena, religion excepted, since we shall return to that later. Its relationships with law and custom, with economy and aesthetics, and also with language, however fascinating they may be, do not concern us here. Between these types of facts and magic we have a mere exchange of influences. Magic has no genuine kinship with anything apart from religion on the one hand and science and technology on the other.

We have said that magic tends to resemble technology, as it becomes more individualistic and specialized in the pursuit of its varied aims. Nevertheless, these two series of facts contain more than an external similarity: there is a functional identity, since, as we pointed out in our definition, both have the same aims. While religion is directed towards more metaphysical ends and is involved in the creation of idealistic images, magic has found a thousand fissures in the mystical world from whence it draws its forces, and is continually leaving it in order to take part in everyday life and play a practical role there. It has a taste for the concrete. Religion, on the other hand, tends to be abstract. Magic works in the same way as do our techniques, crafts, medicine, chemistry, industry, etc. Magic is essentially the art of doing things, and magicians have always taken advantage of their know-how, their dexterity, their manual skill. Magic is the domain of pure production, *ex nihilo*. With words and gestures it does what techniques achieve by labour. Fortunately, the magical art has not always been characterized by gesticulations into thin air. It has dealt with material things, carried out real experiments and even made its own discoveries.

Nevertheless, we could say that it is still a very simple craft. All efforts are avoided by successfully replacing reality by images. A magician does nothing, or almost nothing, but makes everyone believe that he is doing everything, and all the more so since he puts to work collective forces and ideas to help the individual imagination in its belief. The art of the magician involves suggesting means, enlarging on the virtues of objects, anticipating effects, and by these methods fully satisfying the desires and expectations which have been fostered by entire generations in common. Magic gives form and shape to those poorly co-ordinated or impotent gestures by which the needs of the individual are expressed, and because it does this through ritual, it renders them effective.

We must admit that these actions are the prefigurations of techniques. Magic is both an *opus operatum* from the magician's point of view, and an *opus inoperans* from the technical point of view. Since magic is the most childish of skills, it is possibly also the oldest. In fact, the history of technology proves that there is a genealogical link between techniques and magic. By virtue of its mystical character, magic even contributed to the growth of techniques. Magic protected techniques; behind magic they were able to make progress. Magic lent its clear authority and efficacy to those practical, if timid, efforts of the magician-craftsman. Without the support of magic, these efforts and tests would have been considered complete failures and stamped out. Certain techniques with complex objectives, unsure steps and delicate methods—such as pharmacy, medicine, surgery, metallurgy, enamel work (the last two are the heirs of alchemy)—could not have survived, unless magic had proffered help and made them last by actually absorbing them. We feel justified in saying that medicine, pharmacy, alchemy and astrology all developed within the discipline of magic, around a kernel of discoveries which were purely technical and as basic as possible. We hazard the suggestion that other more ancient techniques, simpler perhaps and separated at an earlier stage from magic, were also merged into magic at the very beginnings of mankind. Hewitt tells us that the local clan of the Woivorung, apart from owning a flint quarry where tribes in the vicinity come to get their tool supplies, also furnish the bard-magicians. This fact may be a fortuitous one. Nevertheless, it seems to shed some light on the way our first tools were invented and made. We feel that techniques are like seeds which bore fruit in the soil of magic. Later, magic was dispossessed. Techniques gradually discarded everything coloured by mysticism. Procedures which still remain have changed more and more in meaning. Mystical virtues were once attributed to them.

They no longer possess anything but an automatic action. Likewise, in our own time, medical massage has taken over from the tricks of the bone-setter.

Magic is linked to science in the same way as it is linked to technology. It is not only a practical art, it is also a storehouse of ideas. It attaches great importance to knowledge—one of its main-springs. In fact, we have seen over and over again how, as far as magic is concerned, knowledge is power. But while religion, because of its intellectual character, has a tendency toward metaphysics, magic—which we have shown to be more concerned with the concrete—is concerned with understanding nature. It quickly set up a kind of index of plants, metals, phenomena, beings and life in general, and became an early store of information for the astronomi-cal, physical and natural sciences. It is a fact that certain branches of magic, such as astrology and alchemy, were called applied physics in Greece. That is why magicians received the name of φύσικοι and that the word φυσικός was a synonym for magic.

Magicians have sometimes even attempted to systematize their knowledge and, by so doing, derive principles. When such theories are elaborated in magician colleges, it is done by rational and individual procedures. In their doctrinal studies magicians tried to discard as many mystical elements as they could, and thus it was that magic took on the character of a genuine science. This is what happened during the last period of Greek magic. 'I wish to give you an idea of the mind of the ancients', said the alchemist, Olympio-dore, 'to tell you, as philosophers, they spoke the language of philosophers and applied the tenets of philosophy to their art by means of science.' καὶ παρεισηνεγκαν τῇ τεχνῇ διὰ τῆς σοφίας τὴν φιλοσοφίαν. (Olympiodore, ii, 4; P. E. M. Berthelot, *Coll. des anciens alchimistes grecs*, Paris, 1887, i, p. 86.)

It is obvious that a certain section of science has been elaborated by magicians, particularly in primitive societies. Magicians, who were also alchemists, astrologers and doctors in Greece, India and elsewhere, were the founders and exponents of astronomy, physics and natural history. It is possible to suppose, as we did for technol-ogy, that other, more simple sciences, had similar genealogical connexions with magic. Mathematicians certainly owed a lot to researches carried out concerning magic squares and the magical properties of numbers and figures. This treasury of ideas, amassed by magic, was a capital store which science for a long time exploited.

Magic served science and magicians served scholars. In primitive societies, sorcerers are the only people who have the leisure to make observations on nature, to reflect and dream about these matters. They do so as part of their profession. It is possible to believe that it was also in these schools of magic that a scientific tradition and methods of intellectual scholarship were developed. In the lower strata of civilization, magicians are scholars and scholars are magicians. Shape-changing bards of the Australian tribes are both scholars and magicians. So are the following figures in Celtic literature: Amairgen, Taliessin, Talhwiarn, Gaion, the prophets, astrologers, astronomers and physicians, who seemed to have gained their knowledge of nature and its laws from the cauldron of the witch Ceridwen.

Though we may feel ourselves to be very far removed from magic, we are still very much bound up with it. Our ideas of good and bad luck, of quintessence, which are still familiar to us, are very close to the idea of magic itself. Neither technology, science, nor the directing principles of our reason are quite free from their original taint. We are not being daring, I think, if we suggest that a good part of all those non-positive mystical and poetical elements in our notions of force, causation, effect and substance could be traced back to the old habits of mind in which magic was born and which the human mind is slow to throw off.

We are confident that, for this reason, we shall find magical origins in those early forms of collective representations which have since become the basis for individual understanding. Thus, as we said in the beginning, our work has not been merely a chapter in religious sociology, but is also a contribution to the study of collective representations. General sociology may even gain some profit—and we hope this may be so—since we believe that we have shown, with regard to magic, how a collective phenomenon can assume individual forms.

Index